## Praise for Bill Arnott's Books

"Witty, well-read, and effortlessly entertaining, Arnott may just be the perfect travel companion."
—Thomas Lundy, *Canadian Geographic*

"Bill Arnott enlivens yet another part of the world I love, riding ferries with poetic prose and striking visual art in *A Season on Vancouver Island*."
—Grant Lawrence, bestselling author of *Adventures in Solitude* and *Return to Solitude*

"Arnott weaves an eloquent and delightful tapestry of sights, sounds, and scents arising from the Island earth. Indigenous histories and places are woven intricately throughout, creating a sense of timelessness."
—Cheryl Alexander, award-winning author of *Takaya: Lone Wolf*

"Descriptions of landscape and place are unreal! I was totally captured."
—Bruce Kirkby, author of *Blue Sky Kingdom: An Epic Family Journey to the Heart of the Himalaya*

# A SEASON IN THE OKANAGAN

# A SEASON IN THE OKANAGAN

## BILL ARNOTT

RMB

Copyright © 2025 by Bill Arnott
First Edition

For information on purchasing bulk quantities of this book, or to obtain media excerpts or invite the author to speak at an event, please visit rmbooks.com and select the "Contact" tab.

RMB | Rocky Mountain Books Ltd.
rmbooks.com
@rmbooks
facebook.com/rmbooks

Cataloguing data available from Library and Archives Canada
ISBN 9781771607247 (softcover with flaps)
ISBN 9781771607254 (electronic)

All photographs are by Bill Arnott unless otherwise noted.

Copy editor: Kelly Laycock
Proofreader: Peter Enman
Design: Lara Minja, Lime Design

Printed and bound in China.

All rights reserved. No part of this publication may be reproduced, stored in a retrieval system, or transmitted in any form or by any means – electronic, mechanical, audio recording, or otherwise, including those for text and data mining, AI training, and similar technologies – without the written permission of the publisher or a photocopying licence from Access Copyright. Permissions and licensing contribute to a secure and vibrant book industry by helping to support writers and publishers through the purchase of authorized editions and excerpts. To obtain an official licence, please visit accesscopyright.ca.

We acknowledge the financial support of the Government of Canada through the Canada Book Fund and the Canada Council for the Arts, and of the province of British Columbia through the British Columbia Arts Council and the Book Publishing Tax Credit.

For Dad

# BRITISH COLUMBIA

---

**OKANAGAN VALLEY**

Kelowna
Osoyoos

# OKANAGAN VALLEY

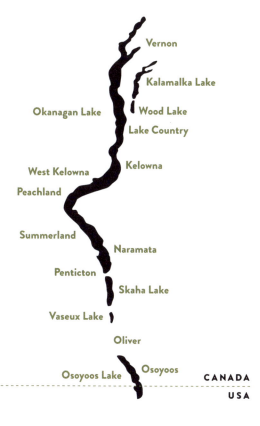

# CONTENTS

| | |
|---:|---|
| 1 | Introduction<br>*The Deep Landlocked Fjord* |
| 5 | First Spoken Language |
| 9 | Same as Hummingbird Wings |
| 24 | Syilx of the Okanagan Nation |
| 32 | Pelmewash Parkway |
| 39 | Toward Vernon |
| 47 | Home of the Countess |
| 68 | Fat of the Lake |
| 72 | The Myth Known as Ogopogo |
| 79 | Heart of the Okanagan |
| 85 | Four Separate Seasons |
| 104 | Geological Events Overlap |
| 111 | The Vibe of the Place |
| 117 | Around Naramata |
| 124 | A Series of O's |
| 142 | Nk'Mip Land |
| 148 | Dobrý den |
| 153 | Cultural District |
| 165 | The Mission and Father Pandosy |

| | |
|---|---|
| **180** | Sncəwips |
| **186** | Lake Music and Ash |
| **191** | Conclusion<br>*A New Gust of Breeze* |
| | |
| **193** | A Note about Names and Narration |
| **197** | Acknowledgements |
| **199** | About the Author |

# INTRODUCTION

---

*The Deep Landlocked Fjord*

**Sun lifts from a low eastern hill,** a warm honey ooze that seeps down the slope to settle on shoreline, then lake. The surface shifts from ebony blue into emerald. One moment more and the water's Olympian, a bronzy glimmer of silver and gold, leaving the deep landlocked fjord surrounded in dusty brown green, to reflect a shimmering sky.

The stretched crook of water has lain in the valley since before the First Peoples arrived, before coyote, salmon, or bear. Gradually, life prospered – bitterroot, saskatoon berry, ponderosa and maple, bunchgrass and cacti, with sunflowers bursting in lemon – as the lake, this last remnant of glacier, made its arduous way to the south before turning west, to meld with a slow-rising sea.

Seasons transpire. And a boy wakes in his bed, the first sound of the day a mourning dove. Its melancholy *ah-ooo-ooo-ooo* emanates from above the boy's home, a compact house nestled next to the lake. Despite the sorrowful timbre and pulse, it's a soothing song to the boy. A comfort. Something he associates with a Sunday.

Dad will be home, working in the yard overlooking the lake. They can swim when Dad's done pruning trees. Mom will spend the morning at service, her church group just down the road. Maybe a sour-cherry pie for dessert. Ladders will come out, after the lawn gets mowed. Plastic buckets. Clamber, balance, and stretch as the deep crimson fruit is plucked from the outermost branches until buckets brim, stained with claret-hued juice. He can taste it already, filling his small body with pleasure. If the call of the dove had a flavour, it would taste of those cherries. The sweet and the sour a succour.

Tiptoeing from bed, the boy cuts through the kitchen, creaks past the screen door, the lake bevelled in sapphire and diamond. Rising sun warms the fruit trees, evergreens, nut trees, and Oregon grape. An aroma of ponderosa. The whirr of a hummingbird vibrates the air, and the boy smiles as it floats before him, the bird's head iridescent, cocking left and then right as though scrutinizing. The boy mimics the bird, angles his head, causing the bird to retreat, then zoom forward, finding focus in space. One more endless pause, a hitch and a fold in time as the boy and the hovering bird gaze at each other, until the hummingbird zips from view. The boy certain, somehow, the little bird is kin to the lake. That

• INTRODUCTION •

sense of connection he'll carry for life, leaving the boy, then the man, to believe that intangible essence must be something quite real. Knowing in his way that, just like the bird, he and the lake are related as well.

A few decades pass and a man eavesdrops on the squawk of two ravens, conversing in rasps. The caws shift in tone, from throaty to nasal. As always the man longs to know what it is they discuss, the avian news of the day. And he satisfies himself by eavesdropping on babble, knowing it's anything but.

He picks his way between cedar and fir to emerge on a road with no cars, trees encroaching on blacktop, creating a tall slender corridor. And there, at head height, framed by trees, a hummingbird whirrs in low sun, the same iridescence he remembers from childhood. An energy hum the man feels when he dreams of his father, the lake, a sensation electric and grounding. Another stoppage in time as the bird hangs, midair, locking eyes with the man. Sun strikes evergreen boughs, resembling wings, the sky overhead, lake blue. The man smiles. His hovering friend, his relation, repeats the dance from their past: feathered head tilting left, tilting right, floating back, zooming forward again. Then the little green bird disappears into canopy, leaving the man on his own – yet far from alone – to savour his return to the now. ❦

# FIRST SPOKEN LANGUAGE

The now brings me back to this area named for its first spoken language. nsyilxcən. Okanagan. And the body of water called kłúsx̌nítkw. Okanagan Lake, or Lake Okanagan. It centres this broad glacial valley, running mostly north–south with a jog partway down, creating a continuous freshwater shore that boasts an endless array of sunrises, sunsets.

As you've no doubt deduced, I am that boy. And the man. Although Vancouver is where I reside, the Okanagan is my original home. Where I spent the first 20 years of my life. Next to that watery spear, piercing the heart of the region.

Having spent a season on Vancouver Island, which I've shared in a previous book, I found in that region another new home. The island now as much a part of me as memories of growing up by the long, crooked lake in south-central British Columbia. Although Lake Okanagan dominates the interior valley, countless pools and ponds accompany the dominant body of water. Kalamalka and Wood lakes, Skaha, Vaseux, and Osoyoos. Not to mention high and low tarns, home to sunfish and trout, a few bass and perch, thick scaly carp, and pink-fleshed, landlocked salmon called kokanee.

The season I spent on Vancouver Island and its myriad archipelago happened organically. Having come to the area for a five-week sojourn, it took three months to return to the mainland. Work-from-home made it possible. Accommodations that were never quite full. So together with my wife, Deb, we just carried on. I'd been handed the brainchild of writing about it by Don Gorman, head of Rocky Mountain Books. Sent on my way with a roll of the dice, passing GO and not looking back.

Now I'm doing it again, only this time I was asked in advance. A tour not planned but envisioned. A loosely pencilled agenda, knowing the area I want to explore, key sites that I'd like to experience, and yet, entirely flexible. A true road trip, open-ended and unconstrained. The way I prefer to explore, finding magic when it's most unexpected.

I've chosen to start with a flight to Kelowna, rent a car to explore, tracing lakes north to south, then back again. And to overlap autumn equinox, the result a span of two seasons. On my way to Vancouver airport, grabbing last minute things for the trip, I'm in a store when I overhear a conversation between shoppers.

"Any plans for the long weekend?"

"Yeah, going to the Okanagan."

• FIRST SPOKEN LANGUAGE •

"Nice."

"Yeah. Hopefully not too hot."

"It can get pretty hot, alright."

"And smoky."

The two nod in silence, knowing that smoke can be the least of the area's worries. Sure enough, fire would soon engulf much of the region, destroying property and livelihoods. Devastating blazes, yet by no means unprecedented. Despite shifting climates, greater intensity and frequency, fire has been part of the landscape for a very long time. Arid climate, grass hills, stands of resiny pine, and lightning strikes that punctuate the dry season.

This plays in my mind as I sip coffee and gaze through a window, now at the airport. As though staring into a campfire, recollective and dreamy. I've chosen this season, or more accurately seasons, not only for agreeable weather but significance too. What hotels and campsites call "shoulder season." Meanwhile, through the glass, the view is shoulder-like too. An in-between sky, hyphenated and tentative. A pre-sunrise blush with robin's egg blue. Wisps of nimbus, a teasing of rain, with a heat-haze hung on horizon. The corridor beyond is a bustle of travel, lineups for food and for gates. Outside, luggage trolleys zip by, flashing yellow in cautions. "I'm Going Home" purrs from a stereo, overdubbed by the hum of espresso machines. A utility vehicle goes past, taillights flashing, a real-life version of Lego I had years ago: a plane, a tiny suitcase. Through the humanity hum, "I'm Going Home" crescendos, as clouds dissipate in the distance. ✤

# SAME AS HUMMINGBIRD WINGS

**My view at the moment** is out a scratchy plane window, as landscape slides by, west to east. Alpine ponds. Smears of cirrus. Razorback peaks. Scrims of snow and avalanche scabs. Undulations of vapour and turboprop blur the same as hummingbird wings. The plane banks, adjusting toward rising sun. Swathes of conifer, clearcut, a gradual shift into khaki, a valley, and finally, the lake, where ripples could pass for a motorboat wake. Or the spirit of a watery serpent.

*"Please ensure seatbelts are fastened and refrain from using the washrooms."*

The inevitable warm-front descent to the long lakeshore valley, always an airborne jostle. Overhead bins vibrate and rattle, grunt and complain. Below I spy dirt capillaries, game trails, and ancient footpaths. Residual wildfire smoke clings to a ridge, adding sepia tones to the blue of the sky, a shawl of cirrus and fug.

The plane's mostly empty and I visit with Doug, my seatmate across the tight aisle. A commercial pilot for the past 30 years, Doug crosses the dateline, doing the Vancouver-to-Sydney run. His home is in Okanagan Mission, part of Kelowna. And I ask him about recent fires.

"Oh, we're fortunate," he says, with a tilt of his head. "We're down by the lake. And the fire was over the hill. It never got close to us. But we have property in Vernon, and the fire there was a half-mile away. A real firestorm. Flames 200 feet high."

I wince.

He nods. "Too close."

I ask him about his commute.

He smiles. "This is my drive home."

I do the math. Doug's been at work for over 24 hours, all of it happening today, yet it's barely eight o'clock in the morning.

Our fuselage shudders, landing gear drops, and we descend as turboprops roar. A soft bounce on tarmac, squeal of black rubber, and a new season is now underway.

I have a small pack with a few necessities, my stuff-sack a reminder of back-to-school days. Transitional season. Crisp and chill at sunrise yet the temperature always crept up, until whatever it was I'd pulled for school would leave me perspiring. Jeans, T-shirt, and sweater, which became a descriptor. Cold mornings and hot afternoons. Days exactly like this.

There's no car for me (yet), so I find a new window and keep drinking coffee.

"You flying out? Getting in? In transit?" a server named Ginger asks as she refills my cup.

"Just arrived. Now waiting for a car."

"Nice."

The coffee's strong, rejuvenating. Outside, hanging planters move in a southerly breeze, pansies and violets like dangling earrings.

I ask Ginger where she's from.

"I live just over there. Dilworth Mountain. I like it."

"Were you affected by the fires?"

"No, fortunately I was on the Island, visiting my mom, in Victoria. I just stayed. The airport here was closed. Only open at night, after dark. They needed it for the water bombers."

"You like it on the Island?" I ask.

"Oh, yeah," she says. "I grew up there. Went from Victoria to Nanaimo, then Calgary, now here. Been three years now."

"And how's that?"

"Oh, it's good. I like it."

A narrative overlap, and I feel even more at home.

That risk of being stranded was how I felt years ago, much like this, flying into Kelowna. Visually, the valley around the airport resembles a half-pipe, a place for giants to skateboard. On our descent at that time, another season of fire, it felt as though we were

• A SEASON IN THE OKANAGAN •

Flight to Kelowna

being dropped into a war zone. Acrid smoke covered the curve of the land. Charred hills had the look of volcanic terrain, the valley resembling Hades.

On that trip I ventured out to a rise, perched between Okanagan and Kalamalka lakes, where a burn was occurring with no visible fire, only

• SAME AS HUMMINGBIRD WINGS •

smoke, ablaze underground. I joined a few people to watch from a lookout. Where Spitfire-like bombers dropped fire retardant, battling the smoulder and heat, the sound of plummeting planes a bone-rattle whine. Again firefighters were victorious. Once more we felt lucky.

From there I hiked another ridge between lakes, with a view of both bodies of water. Okanagan, deep blue; Kalamalka, teal green. Sun lolled in descent as a gibbous moon rose. And I was aware of crunching underfoot, as though traipsing on toasted cereal. Then I realized I was walking on moss. Moss so dehydrated it was disintegrating into powder, an acreage of tinder. Down the slope, ponderosa pines were dropping their cones, preparing for an imminent burn. An uncomfortable place to be. Visually arresting, but raw, vulnerable, foreboding. Within days much of the area burned. Again, fires were contained, damage much less than it might have been. Another season of heroes and lifesavers. ♣

Wood Lake Shoreline

Chiefs Black Bear and Bitterroot

Canoe, Lake Country

North Okanagan Ranch

Dropped Cone, Fire Ready

# SYILX OF THE OKANAGAN NATION

---

**A friendly agent** from the car rental place has tracked me down, passes me keys, and points me toward the parking lot, where a white SUV is waiting. Despite having booked the smallest, cheapest car available, the agent feels bad for making me wait, and I now have a rather luxurious beast from which to navigate the new season.

But first, the lake. Its seasons and people. Indigenous inhabitants of this region are the Syilx of the Okanagan Nation, a tribe spanning the 49th parallel in multiple Bands, sharing common culture, customs, and the nsyilxcən language. Within British Columbia are the Okanagan, Osoyoos, Penticton, Nicola, and Similkameen Bands, along with the Westbank First Nation. The Colville Confederated Tribes of Washington state complete the united Syilx Okanagan Bands.

For as long as the Okanagan have lived on this land, the turn of season has been recognized by the Four Syilx Food Chiefs: two feminine, Bitterroot (spitlem) and Saskatoon Berry (siyaʔ); and two masculine, Salmon (n'tyxtix) and Black Bear (skəmxist). Throughout all of this, Coyote, or snk'lip, the Syilx spiritual guide, looks on.

Seasonal shifts corresponding with food and their Chiefs have an intrinsic, natural patter. Bitterroot in spring, when taproots ripen for picking, their flowers pink, white, and lavender. The roots appear dead through the cold of winter, from which the plant derives its botanical name, *Lewisia rediviva*. Rediviva meaning revival. When spring shifts to summer, saskatoon berries appear in the valley. As well as being a Syilx food staple, eaten both fresh and dried, the deep purple fruit resembling blueberries are used in ceremonial celebrations.

In autumn, time of Chief Salmon, food gathering becomes a priority. Fruit is succulent, plentiful, and game tends to be most abundant. Salmon are running, heading inland to spawn, the primary cultural food representing what comes from the water. Whereas winter, the season of Black Bear, represents balance of all living things, a time of warm winter homes, ceremony, sharing, and gratitude. Within each season an inherent awareness of surroundings, from the ground – above and below – to bodies of water and sky. An almost circadian rhythm as it pertains to an annual cycle, a tidal ebb-flow in the pulse of the planet.

• A SEASON IN THE OKANAGAN •

For my time here, a new excursion to an old and familiar home, this straddle of two calendar intervals will allow me to watch a baton changing hands. From summery Chief Saskatoon Berry to autumnal Chief Salmon. A hybrid endeavour personally as well, with one foot in the past, toe-dipping in memories, another right here and right now. Eager to experience this new season, or two, and to share it again in this manner.

With a deep dive in research, I've come to learn of the Okanagan's geological history, what I consider an album of the land before people. In brief, here's how this valley was formed. A hundred million years ago, when dinosaurs criss-crossed the continent, volcanic islands were shoving their way from the sea to the coast, like land-boats ramming the shore. This pushed the mainland east into crimps, ripples of earth accumulating in hills and building to mountains. When those pushy Pacific isles ran out of steam, the land breathed a sigh of relief, the relaxing terrain then cracking in rifts, one of which is this valley that houses the long, doglegged lake.

The Earth's surface, mind you, varies in thickness. And eventually fiery magma burst through, resulting in high blisters dotting this same stretch of land. Now, some of the most dramatic Okanagan mountains are in fact ancient volcanoes. Water followed, rivers finding low faults, leaving a topography of channels and silty deposits. This erosion continues, with accumulations of rock, sand, and silt slowly shrinking each body of water in the valley.

My research plays out like an old film cliché, pages blown from a calendar, time passing at speed, to about two million years ago. Global temperatures drop and glaciers fill this same space, shifting ice, rock, and water in a scouring effect to reshape the land yet again. The end of that ice age creates the long lake and, by extension, the childhood home for a lot of us.

It's that calendar spin that conjures an array of seasonal representations linked to the land and to weather. I'm reminded of history lessons, where ancient Greeks labelled seasons to correspond with the winds, derived from their gods called Anemoi. A kind of meteorologic forecaster too, as each point on the compass had predominant gales, combined with an element: earth, water, air, or fire. This is why, in part, we still refer to weather as "the elements."

To Mediterranean ancients, each seasonal gust had a god. Boreas brought winter and cold from the north, its element, earth. The promise of springtime and summer belonged to Zephyrus, warm western breezes linked with the water. As the season eased into autumn, southern Notus took over, the element of air, darkening gusts that shoved summer aside and brought storms. Leaving Eurus, the last of the avatar winds. Its element, fire. Because Greece only has three notable seasons, the wind of fire never had its own calendar home, and so could arrive anytime, direction unsettled and vague. Disgruntled and surly, the fire wind often spelled trouble, occasionally looking to fight.

My association with fire, therefore, is a muddle of emotions. The smell of woodfire in a hearth an aroma that comforts, as my childhood home had a fireplace. We'd chop and stack wood at this time of year, in the summer and fall, tree trimmings or logs from a farm. Ideally hardwood, slow burning and warm, the occasional crackle of pitch. Or the soft smoke and low flame of campfire, a cooking surface for fish or marshmallows. Mesmerizing, the dance of orange flame, occasional evergreen sparks. The smell clung agreeably to clothing and hair. Added fragrance to supper, ensuring whatever we cooked was delicious. After food it became the main show, as though watching a stage performance. A version of grass dance, the hiss of visual song. Quite the opposite to the fear felt when wildfire creeps toward town. I could imagine seers coaxing wind to cooperate, moving elements to where they were needed, finding that balance of safety and nature while living amidst it all.

In addition to being here for the seasons of Chiefs Saskatoon Berry and Salmon, it's a time of winds changing as well, when warm Zephyrus breeze turns to the chill blasts of Notus. No doubt the stories I've been reading about wind, its study and documentation, triggered this memory. One I associate with being a child, growing up here, and embracing new mechanization.

The tape recorder was a family gift. For Christmas. Something that appeared under the tree with a gift tag to all of us. Meaning, a high-ticket item. It was a hand-held, portable cassette player. Play, fast forward, rewind. And record. A tiny, magic red button that brought technology into our home, enabling us to, well, record. Anything! We taped songs being played on the radio. (Copyright law hadn't come this far north, as far as I know.) The tape player held a single cassette. So, no tape-to-tape. Or mix-tapes. Just recording the things that we heard. A small microphone plugged into the side of the player. Flick the switch on the mic, press the magic red button, and we were suddenly DJs and chroniclers. Recording all kinds of sounds.

It took no more than a week to realize we could also keep record of farts. Which quickly turned somewhat competitive. Volume. Duration. Vibrato. The recorder itself was by no means high tech. You recorded a sound or you didn't. There was no editing, splicing, erasing. Just a noise caught on tape, or not. And in the same manner a musician will tell you it's not just the notes but the silence between that transforms sound into music, so too did the funniest captures on our playlist of gas become those moments of blank recording. The sound of the mic turning on. Anticipation. Perhaps the soft sound of a strain. Then nothing. With the sad click of a mic being turned off in silent defeat. We even gave our collaborative recording a name. "Storm over the Okanagan." Of course creative differences arose, and the group went separate ways. But I like to believe we've maintained varying levels of solo endeavours in the milieu.

With these warm memories of flatulent gusts, I head out, eager to find an opportunity to put my newfound knowledge of wind, *actual* wind, into practice. I even learned a new word: *psithurism*. The sound of breeze passing through leaves. And the difference between anabatic, or upslope winds, and katabatic, winds that blow downhill. An example of the latter are the "Chinooks" that blast east of the Rockies, pushing temperate air onto foothills and flatlands, bringing heat in the midst of long winters.

And so, with my pack in the back of the big SUV, I leave Kelowna, making my way toward Vernon, to follow the line of the lake. Driving north on Highway 97, away from the airport, orchards seep into hills. A motorbike races past, a sun glint from its mirror a tiny nova of light. Past the dun of Ellison or "Duck" Lake, a sharp bank of sandstone and pine to my left, road carved like a railway through mountains. I settle on a radio station with the least static, now playing "Mama, I'm Coming Home." A theme, so it seems. Leaving me to wonder how much of this journey I'm choosing and how much is mere flow, an old glacier shoving me on through the valley. ✣

# PELMEWASH PARKWAY

---

**Exiting the highway,** I take the low route abutting Wood Lake. Pelmewash Parkway. What was once a main road now quiet, frontage overlooking the water. This is Lake Country, the communities of Okanagan Centre, Winfield, Oyama. I park and stroll amidst willows hugging the shoreline. Feathers from seagulls drift in late Zephyrus wind, as though I've just missed a pillow fight. High overhead, vultures lurch in strong southerly gusts, as Notus seems eager to move in for the season. A multi-use path hugs the lake, with trailheads spurring to high ground. Flits of indigo appear as tree swallows skim the water and pass through the gold of the willows.

I shift in a shuffling circle, take in surroundings, the day. Thoughts drift like the feathers, slow-twirling on water, as though finding a drain. The blue green of lake and of hills. Sandy cliff face and rock. A scent of lakeside and dirt. And I see all around the same visual as a memento I have from that season on Vancouver Island. Something kept on a desk, at home.

It's a thin slice of tree branch, the size and shape of a coin. Wood etched with a vista: peaked mountains, dense forest. The markings carved in the round have the look of a leathery brand, as though burned into place, resembling a tattoo or scrimshaw. It could be the view from our urban apartment, coastal range over evergreen slopes. Land of xʷməθkʷəy̓əm, Sḵwx̱wú7mesh, and səlilwətaɬ Peoples. The Musqueam, Squamish, and Tsleil-Waututh.

The design on the wood fades at its base, as though framed from below by water. By relaxing my eyes and squinting, the scene shifts, a *trompe l'oeil*. No longer mountains and forest but instead weathered hills behind skyscrapers. As though the horizon has shifted, receding into the distance. If I flipped the disc like a coin, it would capture the passage of time that created these lakes: volcanoes and glaciers, dissolving to what I see now.

When I turn the smooth disc in my fingers, I can feel its grain in skewed rings. The wood's alder, I'm sure. Course outer bark, a palette of deep tangerine. The misshapen rings could pass for a topographical map, a cluster of lines to depict a sharp apex with cliffs to one edge. The other side a gradual ascent, a mountaineer's route to the summit. As though the young branch grew with a prominent side. Maybe reaching for light, or sheltering from seasonal winds.

The first time I contemplated the sliver of wood, I couldn't help myself, I counted the lines. Each ring a variation in thickness and shape, none uniform. In the centre, the imagined topographical acme, rings merge into one. A cluster of about half a dozen, the same number of growth-years I had on those days I awoke to the mourning dove. Counting from the centre, each ring broadens, becomes more defined. In total, the branch has over 50. The same number I'd attained when I waltzed once again with the hummingbird.

The slim slice of alder would've come from a branch growing up and away from the trunk. A tree of this type nearing 60 would be an old sample. And although seemingly similar in a copse, each alder's unique, the only deciduous to sprout tiny catkins, a flowering spike that pollinates on the wind. Every blossom comprised of a single nonbinary sex. The biological term is *monoecious*. Female and male in each individual, plants no different than people.

I can glance at my small alder coin when light shifts and watch elements change, a storm blowing in. What before looked like smudges of snow on the mountains could be surly nimbus, clutching the hills' highest heights. A new glance and all I can see is the water, a lake beneath hills. *This* lake, perhaps. A near silent, welcoming whisper.

Here at Wood Lake the park follows the shore. And I trace a series of sculptures, relaying the land and its stories, created by Indigenous artists Clint George of the Penticton Indian Band and Les Louis of the Lower Similkameen Indian Band. Three statues to acknowledge the Okanagan. The *Four Food Chiefs* are here, facing four compass points, relishing seasonal winds. While the other prominent works, the *Feather* and the *Canoe*, stand by the shore and a cycle path.

Along with the high installations are blond slabs of timber with depictions of pictographs, interpretations of working in harmony with land and with settlers. It all fits. Feathers adrift by the totemic *Feather*. The lofty *Canoe* with a light-clouded sky as a backdrop. I line the piece up for a photo and a jet passes over, a juxtaposed snapshot of modern and ancient, a crochet of people and place.

Yet again the art triggers a memory. For it was here, at a pea gravel bend in the lake, I would launch a canoe to troll with a lure for kokanee. The canoe was bright red. Seats of natural birch, with gunwales of steamed, bent alder. The grain ran the length of the boat, much like the whorls in the thin disc of wood with the shifting etched landscape design. As though my time-travelling coin made of alder had reanimated itself, finding a new iteration.

The canoe hull was moulded Kevlar. Durable. Light. And, I presume, bulletproof. I felt safe in the craft. Easy to launch, land, and carry. On my own I could sling it onto the roof of our vehicle, lash the thing into place and go almost anywhere. What surprises me still is that it was an impulse purchase. I'd gone to an outdoor supply store to buy fishing gear, a few lures, when I saw the red boat overhead, displayed near the ceiling. Giving me, for a moment, a fish's view, peering at the hull from below.

I imagined it moving past, dip of paddle, gentle wake in a vee – a watery love at first sight. I no longer remember if I even purchased the fishing tackle. Simply paid for the boat, complete with two paddles, bought straps, eased it onto our car, jammed foam underneath, and was set. All I needed was a body of water. Fittingly, the first lake to touch the boat was Okanagan. I launched the canoe at a short shallow beach of coarse sand. A rough, pleasing growl as the Kevlar slid over the shore, then a slurp and a glug as the lake grasped the boat and took over.

Positioning myself near the stern, I took a few moments to find my balance, a tentative shaking of hands. And then, equilibrium. The feel of joining a welcoming team. I paddled the shoreline, felt the pulse of the lake, a ripple of boats that passed at a distance, wakes rolling like sea monster tracks. The boat rode like a trained mare, finding familiarity in undiscovered terrain. Then I made it official and took the red canoe home. Set it on grass at a cottage we had at the time. Splashed bubbly wine on the bow to "christen the ship," and gave it a name. *Kuyeil*.

I'd tracked down a woman named Muriel, an Indigenous linguist, her lineage from south of the border, her people the Okanogan, Okanagan kin but spelled with two *O*'s and two *A*'s. It was Muriel's relatives that watched Lewis and Clark pass through to create their sea-boiling saltworks on the Oregon coast. The same geographic conclusion as the lake I was following now.

*Kuyeil* was a word I had found, its definition broad, yet vague. Which was why I was speaking with Muriel, to help focus the etymology. A word, she explained, many Indigenous Peoples might know but few remember, like so many words, representing an array of things depending on usage and context.

We spent time simply talking about heritage, and I asked Muriel for more of her story. Her family tree did indeed flow like the lake, north to south with a lateral jog, only this one veered east. Where her kinfolk melded south Okanogan with Indigenous Peoples of the plains: Lakota, Dakota, and Sioux.

*Kuyeil*, she explained, can be difficult to translate. A term with multiple meanings and interpretations, it was most frequently used to describe calm water, peace, and tranquility. And it could also translate into birdsong, the complex language of ravens or falsetto chirp of a hummingbird. All I could do at the time was smile, knowing the name was fitting, and that the boat had received one more blessing.

And so the red canoe had a name. A personality too. Leaving me with a sense that maybe, just maybe, the boat had known water before. That somehow that inaugural dip in the lake was not so much a first encounter but rather a reintroduction. A new reunion with family tree kin. ♣

# TOWARD VERNON

---

**From the statues** of *Canoe*, *Feather*, and *Food Chiefs*, I'm back in the car going north, but stop at Oyama General Store. One of those wonderful shops that has everything: post office, liquor, camping supplies, fishing gear, ice cream, and groceries. I buy pepperoni, while a woman ahead of me grabs cigarillos, a small orange juice, and very large vodka. It's still early on Sunday and I assume she's off to church.

I take a look through the store's freezer, like rummaging through an old treasure chest. One day I came here after an unproductive day of fishing, determined to take home a meal. And what should I find in the back of the freezer but a frosty hunk of *mahimahi*, the golden-blue fish from Hawaii. How it got here I can't fathom, maybe through the in-store postal service. However, I bought it and, with unprecedented wit, tossed it into my fishing net to cart back to our cottage.

"How'd it go?" Deb asked when I got back from the lake.

"I got *mahimahi*!" I said, hoisting my net like a trophy. Leaving Deb to wonder just how far I had paddled.

From the general store I drive to Gatzke's Farm Market, admiring a collection of old tractors. Displayed through the sprawl of the orchard, it's effectively an open-air museum, a century of agricultural moments and tech captured in husks of machinery.

Now with apples to pair with pepperoni, I carry on north, where Kalamalka Lake, also called Kal Lake, points toward Vernon. Over the rise to my left, Lake Okanagan stretches in both directions. Tapping into my inner mathematician, I find, in a neat twist of numbers, that Okanagan Lake's length in kilometres is the same as its surface area in miles: 135. A vast expanse. Reaching depths that according to some have yet to be found. Now a play space for anglers, wakeboarders, and sailors, the lake has a history matching its dim murky floor, in select secret spots beyond fathom.

A geologist with a preference for precision might insist the lake is no more than 240 metres at its deepest. But a few aging divers involved in the maintenance and repair of Kelowna's old floating bridge (now replaced) are convinced the lake bottom goes deeper. Where monstrous sturgeon allegedly glide, prehistoric and scaly as dragons. More than one wet-suited worker refused to return to the water, leaving the lucrative job to get back to less frightening work, things like deep ocean dives amongst stingrays and sharks.

Of course these stories of murk and of myth fuelled fear every time I leapt in the lake as a child. I'd scan the water for sturgeons, squinting into the depths, imagining them resembling the gaping-mouth shark on a poster I had on a wall. Which I would've torn down and thrown out had it not been so horribly cool, an underwater shot in blurred azure. So instead I would hope for the best, close my eyes at the end of the pier, and jump!

It was next to the lake where I'd hear mourning doves on calm weekends, our yard where fruit trees bore filling for pie. With a series of scoured grass hills just beyond, it was ripe to climb and explore. I was keen to be back, knowing the valley and lake, maybe a dove, and a hummingbird too, were calling me home in their way.

The highway eases down a slope into Vernon, past an army camp and a hospital. It's now midmorning, a mix of blue sky and white cloudy fluffs. A short distance north is the Spallumcheen Valley, marking, more or less, the top of the Okanagan. Beyond lies Sicamous and the Shuswap. But the SUV wants to go west, I believe, so I steer toward the big lake, to that place I remember from childhood.

To start here feels fitting. Not only a tidy north tip on the map, but from a settler's standpoint Vernon is the oldest Okanagan community. Following millennia of Interior Salish inhabitation, Europeans arrived in the 1800s, pursuing the fur trade, precious metal, then the agriculture of ranching and orchards. As in much of the continent, missionaries and the Hudson's Bay Company followed that migrating flow. The town population is about 40,000, which hasn't changed much since I was a boy. Unlike the explosive growth south in Kelowna.

That sliver of history around European settlers and land exploitation could almost be traced in a property survey we had, part of buying a bare land strata lot on the outskirts of Vernon. Over a century of mineral and natural resource rights were delineated in dizzying reams of legalese. If oil or gold or fossils were found, we could well have been in a multi-generational line of prospecting settlers with partial claims that were technically binding. We decided to not plant a garden, nor would I dig for worms.

Few cars on the road at the moment are making the morning space intimate. I pull onto a short side road where my elementary school sits, perched on a slope with lake view. On the field is a lone baseball glove. Forgotten? Abandoned? To my delight a mourning dove calls. Maybe it was always like this, the quiet of Sundays showcasing the bird's aria-purr.

This one emanates from a leafy deciduous, ricocheting from the old school walls.

From here I circle the top end of the lake, past Kin Beach (named for Kin Canada, a secular, non-profit group). This is actually one of two north ends to Lake Okanagan, as the top, the bigger body of water just northwest, resembles a mitt, while this bay is the thumb on a map.

Muscle memory kicks in and I head toward my old home. It's been years since I've driven this road yet I'm certain I could do it blindfolded, each undulation and curve. There's the spot where a neighbour picked me up on my bike in a torrential storm, a fall gale making progress on a single-speed bike impossible. There's where I changed a flat tire on mom's car as a kid, feeling I grew up at that moment. And there's the embankment where our friend rolled his car. Dad and I were first on the scene. Drove him in to Emergency, where they stitched up his filleted hand. It was nearly a year before I could stomach sliced ham.

And there's the old lakeshore property, now divided and filled with two houses. On one side of the lot, beneath my childhood bedroom window, grew a cluster of lily of the valley. A bushel of flowers and leaves where an overhang of concrete created a sun-catch while protecting the plants from the elements. With the window ajar by my bed, I would wake to the smell, lingering in still morning air, a fragrance of blossomy greens. If the song of the dove had a flavour, the smell of the lilies had texture. The feel of oil on canvas, silky smooth. A tactile scent.

What may have been the most prominent landscape feature was a towering ponderosa, a pine that had planted itself and stood on the land when Mom and Dad first made the purchase. Two lots on the water, one of the lake's northern corners, with a long curving shore, a blend of small rocks and sand. Perfect for swimming or launching a small boat. Which we did for many years. Some winters the shoreline would freeze, once or twice the whole lake, three kilometres wide where we lived. Frigid winters with smooth, perfect ice. All we needed to do was clear snow, wide shovels and effort, creating our own private rink. We'd play hockey, of course. Sometimes just skate in circles, the bliss of racing atop water we'd swum in, over meaty dark carp and green clams, maybe a sturgeon or two, as the tall ponderosa looked on.

Getting out of the car I'm happy to see the ponderosa's still here. It must be a hundred years old. Still regal, gazing over the lake. Each neighbouring house has a pier and a boat. The water, shared space. Parkland, in a way, connecting the valley. Magpies float on an updraft and a crow flaps as sun glistens the lake, more gems on display.

Driving back into Vernon, the biggest new building around is the pickleball complex, an indication of demographics. Orchards are twinkling, reflectors to scare off the birds. Neat rows of green could pass for a disco, the gleam an earthly aurora. Starlings swirl over apple trees, a dance to the lightshow, perhaps. A fruit stand, a big one with ice-cream, groceries, and rides, shares land with a honey farm, its structure the colour of buttercups. Next to this, Hereford and Angus cattle graze beside fences with two monstrous bulls under cottonwood trees. Cyclists stop for a view of the valley, next to a dilapidated barn and a warehouse. Breeze gusts from the south, a bluster of seasons and gods.

I pass a pink house on a corner, unchanged for 50 years. There's the supermarket parking lot that served as the community centre, a meeting place for teenagers in cars, a place to visit and do donuts. The same Chinese buffet, the same hanging planters with flowers. A new crosswalk, bright with a rainbow. Where three banks once stood there's now one. And I park by a bench with a plaque to my dad. *Loved by the town that he loved.* Today the bench is draped in a leathery man, asleep in hot sun, his face content.

Compelled to complete a pilgrimage I didn't realize I'd begun, I drive to Vernon cemetery, where I find the headstones of mom's parents. Next to them lies their son, my uncle, while another of mom's brothers is buried nearby. It's a peaceful enclosure, bordered in trees. Birdsong thrums, and I experience psithurism as warm currents shuffle the leaves.

It was somewhere in the middle of that alder wood's growth, when I was about 20, that I had a vivid dream of the couple lying under these headstones. My Ukrainian grandparents. Baba and Dido. English was their second language, our communication uncomplicated. Stories with select nouns and verbs, laughter and smiles, an abundance of home cooking. When the dream surfaced, midway through sleep, my late Baba and Dido were there. Communicating to me, in a manner. Dido was writing in a clear script he didn't possess while alive. Letting me know that everything was all right, that the two of them were okay. Baba was there, watching as he wrote out the message, smiling her broad, warm smile. The feel of a hug, same as the food she'd prepare. A penetrating, comforting love. ✿

# HOME OF THE COUNTESS

---

**Although a far cry** from Baba's home cooking, from the cemetery I veer into town for a meal, making an obligatory stop at Dairy Queen, which is how I began the previous Vancouver Island excursion. Next to the drive-thru, an endless freight train moans by, two diesel engines with more boxcars than I'm able to count. Another milkshake, and I move on.

The last time I was here it was well into autumn, a month of dull grey, when I arrived for a writer's residency, an initiative that houses an artist somewhere for a period of time to work on their craft and contribute to the local community. Residencies come with remuneration for the artist, subsidized accommodation or pay. Most often the artist gives back in the form of instruction, offering classes, doing shows or a gig. All of which were part of my residency here. What made the experience unique was the venue where I stayed, a museum on a rise by the cemetery. The former house of Countess Sveva Caetani. Her home was a 100-year-old mansion I had to myself, where I slept in her room, in her bed.

Born in Rome in 1917, Sveva Caetani was the last of Italy's House of Caetani, a 1,200-year family line that included aristocrats, Popes, and Renaissance painters. In 1921, her parents, Ofelia and Leone, knowing they couldn't live in a country where fascism reigned, abandoned their villa and moved here with Sveva, to start a new life in Vernon.

In the midst of their privilege the Caetani fortune dissolved, like much of the world's wealth, in 1929. Sveva's father died shortly after, and a new chapter began. A life of modesty, lived in the mansion. As Sveva grew up, her mother disallowed creativity, forbidding Sveva to engage in the visual art that she loved. So instead Sveva read books, her artistic dreams smothered. But in 1960 Sveva's mother died, leaving Sveva to at last be herself. And to paint. Her output was at once prolific. Vibrant, exotic paintings in fantastical imagery, a lifetime of pent-up creation, unleashed. And I felt both inspired and intimidated to be making my way to her home.

The week prior to my trek to the mansion I was part of a poetry reading, delivering words to a kind group of welcoming misfits. This took place in Vancouver. That evening I was privileged to be on the roster with a Canadian laureate. As we say in the biz, "shared a stage." Which upstarts like me will say when they're part of the same festival as someone of note, never mentioning they're the opening act and that the headliner, say, performed at a separate venue, on the following weekend. All that matters is you "shared a stage" with the star. Or in my case, a small dais with a national treasure.

After sharing the stage, I visited with the headliner, hoping someone might take our photo. Turns out she had just returned from her own residency at the home of the Countess, so I said I was going there next.

"Oh," she said, taking my arm, as though we were now confidants. "Be prepared for her ghost." She met my gaze and lowered her voice. "You *will* meet her ghost."

"Ah," was all I could think to say.

She squeezed my arm, her eyes flinty. "But nothing to worry about. Oh, no. Sveva's lovely. Just fine. Pestered me for a while but I let her know I had work to do." She dropped her gaze, as though concentrating, landing the story through fog. "After the second night I was left alone." She nodded, recollecting. Looked back in my eyes. "You'll be fine. Nothing to worry about. Not a thing." Then she drifted away, a swirl of mystique and hair.

I admit whatever trepidation I was feeling about the upcoming residency, the classes I'd lead, the reading I'd give along with a live performance, paled in comparison to knowing I'd soon be in bed with a ghost.

When I arrived, I took my bag up the wide flight of stairs, Sveva's artwork adorning the walls. Each step groaned, the creak of a century. At the top of the stairs I turned left, down the hall to a sitting room, a kitchen, a closet, then another sharp left to the bedroom. *Her* bedroom. I turned on all the lights. Left them on. Every one. Went to bed in the light, twitching with every sigh in the hardwood, every settling grunt of the house. Outside, a few haunted trees looked on, one gnarly branch tapping the pane of a window. The last trace of day disappeared under overcast sky, turning the house from ashen to charcoal.

It began to snow. Big heavy flakes, drifting in soft silent blankets. Of course all I saw was *The Shining*, a possessed Jack Nicholson trying to downsize the occupants of the house with an axe.

I double-checked all the lights were on. Realized I'd forgotten the one on the stove. Turned it on too. And settled into the bed of the Countess, drifting toward sleep like the snowflakes. Sure enough, Sveva arrived a short while later to peer from the foot of the bed. A neutral expression. As though merely curious, no doubt wondering who was there in her sheets.

Without saying a word, I did what the laureate told me to do, indicated – through thought – that I had work to do, appreciated her space, and her art, and then wished her well, with thanks.

It was the last I saw of the Countess. That was night one. I managed to sleep through the night, and sleep well, I might add. But I spent all of my stay with lights on just the same.

Morning two I awoke to a wonderland. Thick fluffy snow surrounding the mansion in white, piled by trees, blown onto the porch. A proper snow day. But with food in the fridge and reasonable Wi-Fi, I felt suitably prepared. If I thought the first night was silent, apart from the tap of tree branch on window, now the whole world was on mute. I was aware of my breath, visible inside the house, and each creaking step on the hardwood. The only things I could write revolved around silence and solitude, the season and house creating the entire experience. With the Countess seemingly at rest, my only companion was Chief Black Bear, huddled against icy Boreas, autumn long gone, maybe south in the sun with the snowbirds. ✤

Overleaf: Hoodoos, Outside Penticton

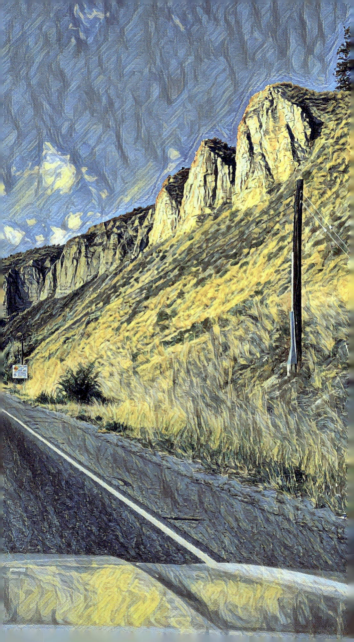

S.S. *Naramata*

S.S. *Sicamous*

Southbound Series of O's

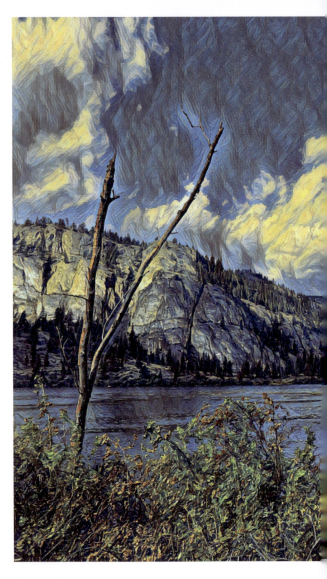

Vaseux Lake

Vineyard, Oliver

Wine Grapes, Oliver

Nk'Mip Chief, Osoyoos

# FAT OF
# THE LAKE

---

Taking my cue from that memory, I turn the car south. Once again I'm on Highway 97, now threading my way between lakes. Okanagan lies west, on my right, with Kalamalka to the east, on my left. On a footpath paralleling the road a bearded man carries a pack, sun illuminating his long flaxen hair, by Kekuli Bay Provincial Park, an arena-like bowl of land fronting Kal Lake. The bight of land is technically a cirque, an open-side hollow in a valley or mountain, the result of glacial erosion. The campsite tucked in the cirque is now thick with trees, although a few years ago it was bare, a vision of landscaping optimism. I recall one of the meatiest supermoons ever, rising over this vista, flooding the hillside in silver.

Today, Kal mimics the surrounding terrain, shades of pine green and spruce blue. A private helicopter sits by a house, idle, as enormous homes brood on the slopes. Oil money from Alberta is evident, with additional wealth from BC's lower mainland and beyond, second (or third) homes with access to ski hills and lakes. North of Vernon sits Silver Star Mountain, while Kelowna has the resort of Big White, famous for long gentle slopes with networks for snowshoes and summertime hiking.

For now the high hills are snowless, a blend of bare brown and treed green. I pass a pond where a sign warns of turtles. Bullrushes sprout from the shore, and I gawk through the deadfalls, scanning for shells with legs. The rental car beeps as I stray, sensors to keep me in line.

To one side of the road, ragged cliffs the colour of marmalade. Granite? Sandstone? The look of old seabed scrubbed clean by shapeshifting glaciers. There's a lonely dead pine with a crook-finger top, pointing out at the lake. I can't help but look, despite another beep from the sensor. What I see is a vista the same as a painting we have, a gift from my childhood friend Danny.

Within the span of a sleepover, Danny became my best friend. Not yet teenagers, we resembled that alder as it reached for the sun. Independent green shoots rooted while splitting from stalks, the mycorrhizal network of youth.

We played Little League baseball together. Danny's dad was our coach. My dad helped as assistant coach, bat-boy, and go-fer. Lines blurred, for me anyway. The roles of mentor, parent, and coach at times were much the same thing. I suspect Dan felt the same way, knowing it to be true when he spoke at my dad's celebration of life. He took the mic to say things that I felt, sharing in a way that I couldn't. Not on that day in that way.

Dan was best man at my wedding, standing beside Deb and me. Years later, when I was alone on a desolate mountain in Greenland, a black storm rolling in, I wondered if the old rules would apply, with Dan needing to marry my widow. Of course we should've run it by Deb, but I was certain she'd be fine with an upgrade. However. What I thought of was the lake and of loved ones, knowing it would all be okay.

Dan's wedding gift was the painting of this view, a piece by Okanagan artist Mary Keith mounted in a simple bronze frame, highlighted in blue. I'm convinced it's the same as the ancient honey-hued sunrise, sliding down the slope to the lake. Only this lake is Kal. A small replica of Lake Okanagan. From above it could be the offspring of the big lake. The same lilt to the east. The same open maw at the top, two serpents mid-speech, facing right. A vista that spoke of a world from which spokes radiate.

Some time later, the scoop-shaped park would sprout from that view. Kekuli. Named for Indigenous pit houses that dotted this space through the seasons of Black Bear, daubed onto canvas years later, then framed and placed on our walls. I say walls because we've had many homes. Not at once but over a number of years. Remarkably, wherever we were the painting would fit, finding the colours of each space. The same tawny tones surrounding the lakes, the valley, the dreams of shared childhood homes.

For two decades we watched the park grow, maples and alders, leaves facing the lake, bracing snowdrifts in winter. It was on our first trip to this discreet archaeological site that we watched that monstrous moon ease into the night sky, the same hills that framed the sunrise but transposed to a film negative hung with a chorus of stars, each lunar dimple made clear. Then we crept to the lake, sidled through low poison ivy, to dunk in mercurial water. ❧

# THE MYTH KNOWN AS OGOPOGO

**The fact that these lakes,** Okanagan and Kal, resemble two slack-jawed snakes has its own fitting narrative. Lake Okanagan in particular, the region's grandaddy of water, has for years been purported to have its own monster, much like the famed Scottish loch. Driving south I'm now between lakes. Okanagan to the west, with Kal, Wood, and Ellison fading behind me. Vernon's long gone from my rearview mirror, and as I approach Kelowna I'm engulfed in a retail stream. While strip malls slip by, I let my mind drift to the lake and its depths, rumours of sturgeons, tales of bottomless murk. And the Okanagan's own Nessie, the myth known as Ogopogo.

Called nx̌a?x̌?itkʷ by the Syilx, Ogopogo represents the Lake Spirit, responsible for preservation and ecological balance. On those occasions when the First Peoples would access or cross the water, a gift would be offered to the Spirit in gratitude, often tobacco, sage, or small game. Legend has it the Spirit could manifest in a serpent-like form, that undulating hill-valley shape much like waves.

Later, non-Indigenous settlers, too, spoke of something, something large and alive, being there in the water. In 1855, Métis settler John McDougall was crossing the lake, his horses tied in a line swimming behind his canoe, when according to him, the animals were pulled under, forcing him to cut the ropes to avoid being dragged down as well. Then in 1872, European settler Susan Allison reported seeing a dinosaur cavorting in the lake. Leading some to believe the creature might be a plesiosaur, an ancient leviathan that had survived through earth tremors and glaciers.

Stories like these perpetuated a Eurocentric notion of a slithery monster living deep in the lake, possibly in underground tunnels that might connect the valley's bodies of water. An alternate interpretation of the Indigenous Lake Spirit, its presence not unlike the Four Food Chiefs, instilling harmonious land relations. Or the Coyote snk'lip, a guide like my SUV sensors, reminders to stay the right course.

On a map, the lake *does* resemble a serpent, jaws agape, set to consume the North Okanagan, as though worming its way from the south. Maybe that image contributed to the settler myth of Ogopogo, a living version of Nazca lines, the giant geoglyphs that adorn the high plains of Peru. Then again, it could simply be how the water can appear in certain conditions. It's easy to see how a person might envision a creature roll at the surface, a glint of hunched back or scaled dorsal. On a few rare occasions I've witnessed a long, lone, and trundling wave, the occasional whitewater break, like fins. With no wind on the water. No boats or other disturbance. Just a long curling ribbon of water, making its way down the lake, a mysterious aquatic nomad, seeking a new domain. Or pacing, having outgrown its boundary shore.

There's a story I'm told is quite true of a local radio announcer in the 1950s reporting a sighting of the lake monster on-air. The announcer went on to encourage anyone with a vehicle to drive down to the beach at the end of the lake and honk their car horns. This, the DJ explained, would attract the beast, and the town could once and for all prove its existence. Imagine what it would do for the tourist trade! Remarkably, a great many motorists did just that – congregated at one end of the lake and blasted away on their horns. Sadly, it did not draw out a monster. But it did result in a story and, as I understand it, a reprimand and a week without pay for the DJ.

The Indigenous legend of the Lake Spirit, however, has location specifics. That its home is near Rattlesnake Island, at the narrow dogleg of Lake

Okanagan and across from the most frequent lake-crossing point for the Syilx, a smooth beach by what is now Peachland, much like the shore where I'd slide *Kuyeil* in the water.

History and mystery reside at this jog in the lake. For it was in the 1970s a man named Eddy Haymour bought the island, a rock lump that resembles a half-submerged egg. Eddy intended to develop the island into a Middle Eastern-themed tourist attraction, ferrying guests from Peachland. Plans included camels, pyramids, and golf. But the provincial government shut Eddy down, citing a convoluted array of issues. Eddy was outraged. He sued. To no avail. Pled his case to the federal government, again without recompense. So he took things to an entirely new level. Going instead to his home country of Lebanon, where he garnered support and seized the Canadian embassy in Beirut. This got the result he was looking for. Following nine hours of negotiation and a nonviolent return of the embassy, Eddy's case was reopened, in which the BC Supreme Court decided he had indeed been abysmally treated, and he was given fair value for Rattlesnake Island. Now known by some as Eddy's Kingdom.

My mind meanders, finding parallel history, people treated unfairly. Displacement. Threats of violence. Hopeful of change, perseverance, and healing. Yet here I am in a bubble, cruising in comfort, savouring sights. Which doesn't feel bad, so I choose not to question, and instead carry on. Plenty to see but plenty of time, no agenda to keep. I had planned to arrive a month earlier, but fires made that impossible. I shifted a hotel reservation, and now I'll stay for a while on the southern part of the big lake. Across the bridge at Kelowna to the land of the Westbank First Nation.

Apart from high shreds of cirrus, the rest of the valley is congested in haze, fresh smoke, and watery clouds. Through this, patches of rainbows appear. No arches, just pockets of colour in ovals and thumbnail smears. An osprey flaps from the lake, riding updrafts into the hills. Anabatic gusts, I presume. Behind me, away to the north, my rearview-mirror perspective becomes a clear canvas, gold hills and tourmaline lake, as though I could step, Narnia-like, into that Mary Keith painting. Around where I've come from is messy cloud sky, a bed left unmade, thrash of quilt cast aside. A single-prop plane jiggles down to an airstrip, the waggle of wings in high wind.

I pass a cheerful industrial building painted yellow, its signage: *Jealous Cherries, World's Juiciest Fruit*. Next to this a forklift shifts huge wooden bins of bright pumpkins, the same marmalade orange as the cliffs by the lake. It couldn't be more autumnal.

Overhead, an abridged skein of ducks seeks the rest of its chevron. I see consonants in spidery flight:

a *W*, *L*, now an *M* and a wonky half-*V*. Teams play on a field while the hill directly behind them has a forest fire currently burning. Life carries on. The edge of the smoke shreds in kaleidoscope hues. A sign reads *Every Drop Counts*, water restrictions in force. A helicopter buzzes the highway, trailing a line with a big water bucket. Wind moves the bucket, making it look like a hypnotist's watch. *You're getting sleepy!*

I find the hotel as sun sinks in a jam of apricot, cherry, and plum. Checking in I meet Ally, a local who knows, so it seems, everything going on in the valley. She lets me know that she's been okay throughout recent fires. And that many guests in the rooms are locals who've lost their homes in the blaze, being housed here by ESS (Emergency Support Services). Their stays are now long-term, month-to-month, while insurers go through the claims.

"We upgraded you to a mountain view," she adds, which I can't quite process, still empathising with families being stuck in these rooms, their stays indeterminate. I feel guilty, fortunate, relieved. An emotional jumble the same as the mottled night sky.

"Thanks," I reply, still not knowing what "mountain view" means. The rise here in West Kelowna seems to be surrounded in mountain. Although I appreciate the gesture, like the big SUV. But I understand once I get to my room, toss my bag on the bed, as the view through the window is serene. Facing north, across the sharp face of Mission Hill bluff. My own little blank canvas Rushmore.

A rambunctious *clump-clump-clump* of tiny feet overhead, the room upstairs, rattles the building. The tired old man in me starts to get cranky until I realize the upstairs guests are almost certainly a newly unhoused family, trying to keep children amused on a school night, here in a highway hotel, as they steel themselves for another day on the phone with adjusters. And with a sigh and new mix of emotion, I hope that the thundering kids are at least having fun. ❖

# HEART OF THE OKANAGAN

**Breakfast included.** It's a new day, and early, when I drag myself to the downstairs buffet, where a few tattooed men are about to ship out to oil rigs in Alberta, along with a foursome of firefighters. I make a mental note to never complain about work, then fill up on "kitchen-sink oatmeal," before visiting with a local named Aeris.

We chat for a while about the area. Aeris came to the central Okanagan as a child, her mom coming from Newfoundland, having gradually worked her way west.

"I've been here since I was this high," Aeris says, indicating her hip. "And I loved it. Seeing the area grow. And the lake! Well, we're spoiled. We take it for granted. But it's beautiful all year. Wintertime too. Now that I'm, you know, *adulting*, it's less exciting. Sure, just four hours to Vancouver, but…"

Outside, a row of silver maple are in mid-season transition, leaves half green and half red. Nearby are tall lilacs and a hedgerow of yew. Sun peers over cumulous, a view of the Mission Hill tower aglow, a citadel topping the lake. And with a sense of adventure, I head south through the valley.

The day's started with light wind and cloud, sun rising in coral. Starlings dart past; there's a raven on foot, and a seagull circles a golf course. Last time I was here I went to see a friend at their ranch by the water, where thoroughbreds grazed by the lake. If I thought a family having to evacuate was a difficult thing, what do ranchers do with a herd of cattle or a stable of horses?

Driving, I see fire-scarred hills, black timber on slopes like discarded birthday cake candles. The road forks. Highway 97C veers west, while I carry on south, where ponderosas dot gravel inclines. A series of signs: south to *Peachland*, *Penticton*, *Osoyoos*. West is *Merritt*, *Kamloops*, and *Hope*.

I'm now in a long line of semis and trailers, with an out-of-place long yellow bus. Slopes abutting the highway shift from orange into pink, while ahead, as land drops, I see nothing but water. The highway continues to dip, mist hangs on the lake, breath from Ogopogo perhaps, or aurora of Eddy's Kingdom, as straight ahead lies Rattlesnake Island.

Breaking on a curving decline, I drive under a sign. *Historic Peachland. Heart of the Okanagan.* Wind picks up, decidedly aggressive. Even the big trees are moving. Another sign indicates I'm 100 kilometres from the American border. There's a hillside of homes and a scraggle of earth, unhealed wounds from landslides. Gusts ripple the lake. A promise of showers beyond, white tufts with dark smears. My radio choices on the FM dial are 97, 98, or 100, as though I could sing a reverse beer-bottle song. I pass neatly tended yards, small orchards and miniature Edens. More maples are turning, and just like the bi-colour hardwoods, even the pines are adorned in a blush of red gold.

Signage points toward wineries. Ravens scrum by a bin. Another yellow bus, a school field trip, the highway now level and straight. An enormous, metal-cast peach tops a pole, a lollypop ripe for a giant. A monster truck rumbles the opposite way. More bullrushes next to the road, oases hiding in ditches. Nearby, some elms. Stands of droopy dry pine hang on slopes. A sign indicates risk of rockslide.

I stop for a stroll through Peachland. A rickety pier takes me onto the lake, where I wobble and stand on the water. And I think once again of the fires. When I opened the car door this morning, a swirl of ash blustered out, a twister from inside the vehicle. I'd been unaware of any ash in the air, but clearly it's here, all around.

Back on the road, I have airborne company. Starlings mimic the vehicle, a flock bearing south, as though I have a small, feathered escort, the road here barely rising above the lake. At this speed it looks like the car is amphibious, skimming the surface, surrounded in twittering birds. South of Peachland, traffic accelerates. No change in speed limit, just an increase in urgency. The road rises, the lake falls away, along with my escort. Clusters of saskatoon berry trees grow in scrawny bouquets, reminders of the summertime Food Chief. I'm now aggressively speeding but still slowing traffic, and I don't understand the radical shift in flow.

I pass a small B&B on the hill, where Deb and I stayed for a hummingbird show, unplanned, a real-life *Fantasia* display. We'd come for two nights and decided to stay close to Peachland at a house overlooking the lake. The sun was setting behind us, washing the evening in rich ribbons, another sky filled with peaches and plums, until it was one shade of indigo, stars awaking in twinkles. Then the show *really* began, as a cluster of hummingbirds danced in the gloaming, whirling in silhouette shapes. They actually hummed, racing in up-and-down streaks, at times more than our eyes could discern. A ballet of dizzying aerodynamics. The result, a feeling of home once again.

I returned sometime later, coming back down that hummingbird hill for a few days in Summerland. Having been selected as one of a dozen Canadian songwriters to spend a weekend working on craft with two Hall of Famers, one a country star, the other a rock and roll icon. Although we'd be there to share songs, it felt like fantasy camp. Based on style, half the group would work with the country artist, while I was amongst the six who'd write with the rocker.

Both our respective mentors, it turned out, were profoundly deaf. Deaf, that is, when it came to conversing. Yet remarkably, in a cacophonous cluster of a dozen guitars (all playing something different), either could pick out a slightly flat note from 20 paces away. A reminder that music is felt as much as heard. Then again, "deafness" may be a defense against fawning fans.

After a couple of days of jamming and tweaking our songs, we were treated to a concert put on for the town by our instructors, taking the stage to do what they do: play and perform and make strangers feel good. The experience was superb and *did* help to springboard my songwriting. But what stands out from then, spliced with chords and harmonics, are visuals of the lake. Always present, through windows past a rolling, treed yard.

The space was the home of the late George Ryga, Canadian playwright, poet, and novelist, his work exploring the experiences of Indigenous Peoples in Canada. His play *The Ecstasy of Rita Joe* is likely his best-known piece. Many consider Ryga's work to be the most important English-language writing about Indigenous culture by someone of European descent.

The play's been performed for decades across Canada, including shows by the Royal Winnipeg Ballet.

It's the story is of an Indigenous woman arriving in a city to find no place of belonging. Homeless and unhoused in every sense of the word. The connection to my musical weekend is that Ryga also wrote influential lyrics that became popular songs, performed by my songwriting mentor in bands that he fronted. Those lyrics brought social awareness to legions of listeners, new light on a timeless dilemma.

On that trip, from a dip in the highway paralleling the lake, I ascended a scowling slope to a fruit stand perched on a cliff. It was still Zephyrus climate, season of Chief Saskatoon Berry. And there, alongside the peaches and plums and a few early apples, was a display of cherry juice the rich colour of garnet. I was offered a sample to taste, the shopkeeper extolling its virtues: antioxidant, healthful, rejuvenating. I closed my eyes. Sipped. And was immediately teleported to childhood, to the mourning dove song and fresh pie. I passed over all the cash that I had and lugged juice to the car. Over the next few days I indulged, gulping like a nomad having just crossed a desert, my oasis a deep cherry red. But I knew that my treasure was finite, and then rationed. A half glass. A shot glass. A thimble. One month later my stash was depleted. I returned to the market, but Chief Saskatoon Berry was gone, along with the cherries and juice. The season had changed, the sour-sweet fading like sunset. ❖

# FOUR SEPARATE SEASONS

---

Something I'd hear growing up, shared with pride, is that the Okanagan enjoys four separate seasons. Each time frame distinct and appealing. From an abundance of apples and pears in the autumn, to snowy winters that keep skiers happy, to sunflowers in spring, to what may be the star of the seasonal show, glorious sunny, hot summers. A time when each lake becomes its own playground, a place for picnics and boating and swimming.

It would be a few years before I learned of the Food Chiefs, that precious land-balance synonymous with seasons, along with ancient settler gods and their elements found on a compass. I still associate this time of year with returning to school, college, a "proper job." Time of transition, impossible to dress for, every item of clothing like Goldilocks's oatmeal. But now, with car windows open, I recognize the season's aroma as leaves turn, changing colour and wilting, eager to melt in the earth. A time of fall fairs and harvest, pumpkins and gourds. Costumes for trick-or-treating.

Then of course winter comes, like that morning in the Countess's mansion. Hiding leaf mulch and overripe fruit that got missed. Ski reports become the most relevant news. Around here it's Mount Baldy, Apex, and Crystal Mountain, with Big White and Silver Star to the north. *Any fresh powder? What's the base?* Updates a skier will live by. In much of the valley, wintertime fog is common. Long cloudy days with grey smears substituting for sun. But the ski hills are often above it, frequently cast in sunshine. Summits and slopes striped with chairlifts and T-bars will poke through the cloud, gifting light in the dim months of winter. In the snow and the cold, mountains trump lakes, becoming the go-to resorts.

In Summerland, I pull from the road, stretch my legs, and enjoy a temperate breeze off the lake. There's an orchard and fruit stand, and I saunter over and visit with a woman named Melinda. All around, wind is moving the fruit trees, the sound a white susurration.

"How do you like it here?" I ask.

"Oh, I love it!" Melinda replies. "Peachland, Summerland. It's just perfect. Four seasons. You can swim in the lake, or, you know, canoe, kayak. Then go and ski in the afternoon." She pauses. "You *do* kind of need to be financially stable, mind you. It's gotten quite pricey in the area."

"The whole valley?"

"More or less. Penticton has gotten quite…" She looks south, searches for the right word. "Eclectic."

"How so?"

"Terrible homeless problem."

"More so than elsewhere?"

"Oh, yes," she nods. "They haven't done anything to address it."

I think of the mansions. The helicopter, essentially another family vehicle in that home. The spread of wineries. Knowing what each bottle will go for. I feel helpless, and angry, and blessed.

It turns out Melinda works here, where the orchard is selling its produce, so I follow her in through displays. There's a stack of boxed cherry juice, and I wonder if I can recapture that essence. This batch was made from sweet Lapins, their juice the same lustre as red wine.

Melinda sees what I'm doing. "I think this year's the best batch ever produced," she says.

"Why's that?" I ask.

"All the sunshine this year. Sun and no rain. The fruit's just packed with sugar," she adds, referring to the cherries' natural sweetness. "Do you know all the health benefits of it?"

I think I do but want to hear more, so I say, "I know it's good for you. That's about it. And that it's delicious."

"Sure is!" she says. "Good for arthritis, and blood pressure. But you may want to cut it with water or club soda." Then she grins. "Sometimes I use vodka as well."

I can't help but laugh. A holistic approach to good health.

Within a few days I'll be visiting friends, so I buy a few boxes for gifts. In front of the orchard, before continuing south, I open one box, recycle a used coffee cup, pour a sample and taste it.

Perfection.

Precisely what I had hoped for. Maybe even what I remember. Regardless, even if recollections have snowballed, this is a fine replication. Memories of fruit-picking ladders, red-stained fingers, and pie. Making me feel that this red-toothy smile might be permanent.

Whether a burst from fresh juice or old coffee, I can't be quite sure, but I feel an adrenaline jolt. The day's lovely and I'm sure I could do this forever. Back on the road, still heading south, I'm nearing the end of Lake Okanagan. The valley has straightened out, north to south, the blue of the lake now with the feel of a dwindling waterhole. Which might be due to the fact I know a desert is just up ahead, which warrants more exploration. But before I reach that, there's much more between here and there.

Despite arid land, moisture clings in the air as late-morning sundogs fan over the lake, where two sprawling campgrounds embrace by the shore. The next road marker, *Penticton, Osoyoos*, leans in a northerly wind. I can hear the metal sign creak, even through closed windows.

Traffic slows to one lane, crawls up the highway, as bulldozers and dump trucks clear a massive landslide from the road. The volume of earth that only recently fell from the mountain to cover the highway is shocking. Another wave of vulnerability. Cars ease to a stop, a long line waiting to access the one open lane, at the same instant Bobby McFerrin starts to coo from the radio. "Don't Worry, Be Happy." I can't help but smile, forget about time, and help Bobby out on the midrange.

Gradually, traffic gets moving again but driving south on the northbound side. On the inner lane, heavy trucks roar past, moving dirt at double or triple our speed. Ahead, a blanket of wineries, golf courses, stands of sumac and birch. More sundogs, their palette shifting to blue. I can make out George Ryga's home. Memories of songwriting, a blend of isolation and sharing. ❧

Kettle Valley Railway

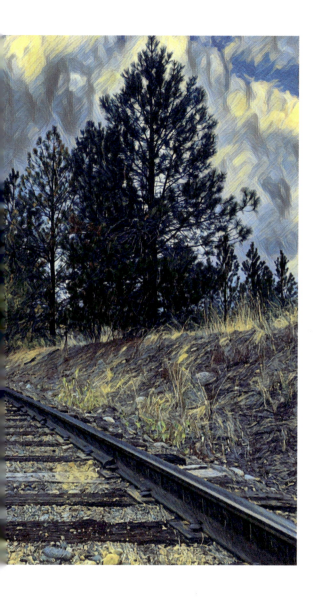

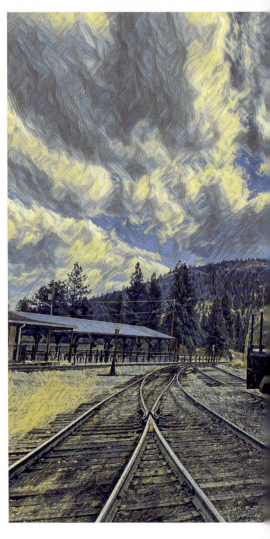

KVR, Summerland

Desert Cactus

Kasugai Gardens, Kelowna

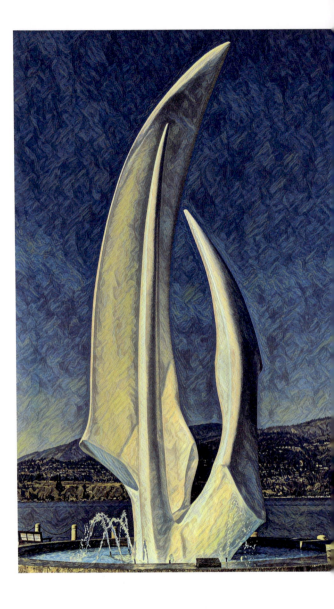

*Spirit of Sail*, Kelowna

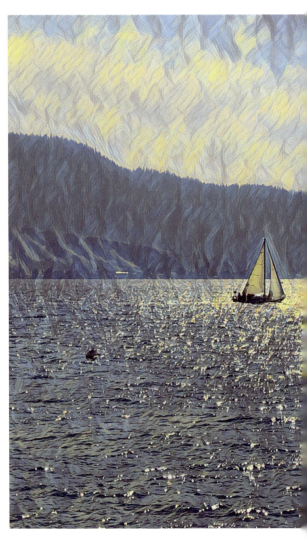

Sailing on Okanagan Lake

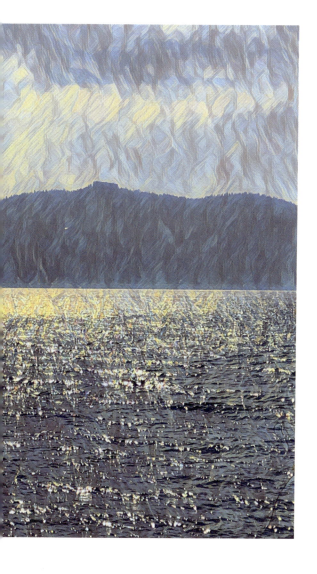

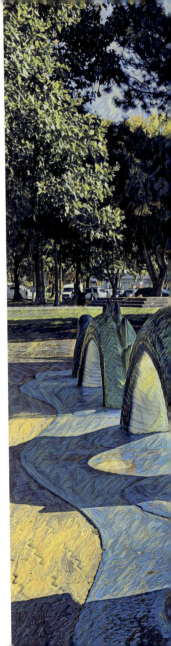

Ogopogo, Tourist-Style

# GEOLOGICAL EVENTS OVERLAP

**The intimidating profile** of Giant's Head Mountain stands dead ahead. An ancient stone feature in which geological events overlap, this 500-metre igneous crag was one of the original valley volcanoes, but one that spewed multiple times through the mantle, in what are called lava bombs. An earthy version of fireworks that explode and then re-burst into fresh iterations.

Circling the base, I lack the motivation to climb but can see that the area offers vast views around Summerland. South is Penticton. The small town of Naramata is just across Okanagan Lake, along with the golden-green ridges of Okanagan Mountain Provincial Park, now encompassing Rattlesnake Island.

Carrying on, the road jogs and I'm driving into the sun, past dusty hoodoo embankments in taupe and ecru. On the water, near shore, tethered boats bob in the breeze. An osprey preens in a spindly dead tree. More glittering orchards, with tinsel waving in wind. I'm compelled to wave back.

## GEOLOGICAL EVENTS OVERLAP

Steep hoodoos continue, closing in on the highway and lake. It feels like frontier terrain, spaghetti westerns, and vultures. And as if on cue I spy actual vultures circling Pyramid Park, zigging and zagging like kites in high wind. I consider Eddy Haymour's dream to construct his own pyramids, an envisioned resort on the lakefront. The terrain does indeed conjure Saharan imagery. Sharp cliffs and sharp winds. More lopsided raptors. Soorimpt Park is next door. And for the next few kilometres I work at pronouncing the park name, a tongue twister instead of the radio.

A strong gust gives the SUV a rude shove, as beachside high-rises indicate I'm nearing Penticton, where stretchy-wrapped cyclists clump on the roadway. In the distance, a weird blend of dark cloud and smoke, sure signs of fire and rain, making James Taylor sneak into my mind. (For younger readers, Taylor has a song called "Fire and Rain.")

Time for a change, and to purge Taylor's tune from my brain. I pull into Penticton, park the vehicle, and search for a trail. Near a bridge into town, I follow the Penticton River Channel, a canal conduit, picking up both the Trans Canada Trail and KVR, or Kettle Valley Rail Trail. Both of which lead me to town, through a lakeside strip of restaurants, car lots, service stations, motels. A golf course, more inns. I loop my way south, never far from the highway, the river-like channel, and the lakes.

There's the space where a summertime market takes place, a sprawl of artwork and clothing and produce. A sports centre. Some walkers, more cyclists, coming off or beginning the trails. The river flows south, now with the look of a clean-banked canal, tousled in white-flowered hogweed.

Here, Penticton serves as a link. North of town is Lake Okanagan, while south of city centre is Skaha Lake. The gentle flow of the channel connecting the two is a destination for swimmers and sunbathers on tire tubes and foam noodles. The space has the feel of an open-air party, a campground, with some of the floating contraptions resembling sofas, chairs, whole living-room sets, equipped with umbrellas and coolers – the makings for a day on the water.

Strolling the river canal, I break through lupine in mauve, pink, and purple. The water is brisk, maybe the flow or the breeze. Cool to the touch. Aroma of greenery. Strands of milfoil move at the surface, mermaid hair in trusses of green. A few swallows fly by. I head back to the car and, in the shade of a Norway maple, sip cherry juice with a smile.

In the mood for some history, I make my way to a fresh-air museum at the foot of Okanagan Lake, where Penticton looks north up the valley. I'm on a branch of the Trans Canada Trail, a vast network you're likely to pick up all across the country. Also known as the Great Trail, this system of paths connects waterways,

• GEOLOGICAL EVENTS OVERLAP •

greenways, roadways, and trails to link the Pacific, Atlantic, and Arctic Oceans. Spanning the continent, 24,000 kilometres, it's considered "the longest recreational, multi-use trail network in the world."

The Trans Canada Trail, or TCT, is also the name of the non-profit fundraising group that continues to develop the paths, while ownership, operation, and maintenance happens regionally. Now, much of the TCT focus is on increasing accessibility – replacing roadways with greenways, new loops, and spurs – to encourage more users with varied mobility. It's one of those spaces, or initiatives, where you can't help but feel connected. Part of something much grander than any one person or place. A reminder that we're all environ-organisms, integral components of a natural whole.

I return to the tidy confluence of the KVR and TCT, now walking between lakes, Okanagan and Skaha, to eventually arrive at old boats, the museum I'd been heading to previously. Here, on the south shore of Lake Okanagan, next to a bristling rose garden, are the S.S. *Sicamous* and S.S. *Naramata*, ships half in and half out of the water.

The S.S. *Naramata* is a steam tug, first commissioned by the Canadian Pacific Railway. In service from 1914 to 1967, the tug was used to haul barges and dislodge ice in lake harbours, an all-in-one freighter and icebreaker.

The S.S. *Sicamous* is a quadruple-decked sternwheeler, also owned by the CPR, used collaboratively by orchardists in Penticton, Kelowna, and Vernon. Launched in the same year as the *Naramata*, the *Sicamous* only ran until 1937, being beached more or less where it sits in front of me now, part of the heritage park and museum, used occasionally for special events.

Later I'd visit with my niece Melissa, who lived for a while in Penticton and attended Gatsby-themed dinners aboard the *Sicamous*. Modern-day galas recounting past glamour, a fun spin on a gloomy tale. Now, the *Naramata* and *Sicamous* sit side by side, labelled sister ships, grande dames admiring the view. I almost see them as Statler and Waldorf, the elderly Muppets who heckle performers from the comfort of their balcony seats.

The neck-craning sternwheeler also conjures Mark Twain. I can imagine the ship slap-paddling down the Mississippi, kids on the shore whitewashing fences, chewing on straw, and jigging for catfish. An evocative time machine, plunked on trimmed grass by the water.

From the venerable boats I scramble to a promontory of sandy gravel and stone, now in the bite of a rising gale. Looking back at the ships, it takes no imagination to envision them launching into these waves on the lake, where mud hens now bob in a raft on the watery heave.

• GEOLOGICAL EVENTS OVERLAP •

Fighting back through the wind on a reinforced breakwater meshing with beach, I find a low, heavy stone oven. Brick-slabs of rock stacked in an igloo design, an inner hearth made for baking. Although resembling a small model of an Indigenous kekuli home, these little piles of stones were constructed by railroad workers and still dot the CPR line, where builders were ensured fresh-baked bread every day. A remnant of history, discreet archaeology for any sightseer to discover, like turning flour to bread. Simply add equal measures of curiosity and observation.

From the ships and stone oven, I follow the promenade east, skirting the south shore of the lake. Okanagan Lake Park sits at one end of the path, with more railway memories as I cross Van Horne Street, named for William Cornelius Van Horne, overseer of the CPR, the first transcontinental railway, completed in 1885. A steam-driven version of today's TCT.

Aptly enough, I cross KVR-TCT Trail once more, along with the bike route sharing that name. A sign warns cyclists and drivers to *WATCH FOR DEER*. Nearby, crows blacken a field in a hovering airshow. There's a cemetery overlooking the lake, a patch of calm by the water. The main road cuts through orchards and vineyards, climbing a ridge feathered in rattail grass and speckled with dry ponderosa.

There's a small self-serve fruit stand, an empty kiosk next door. And a lookout to Munson Mountain.

This rise of granite is considered one of Canada's Historic Places, home to a gargantuan lettering of PENTICTON, spelled out in white rock on the hillside and commanding this end of the valley. It's designed in the same manner as the HOLLYWOOD sign. Only here, rather than white-painted steel, the local name is comprised of small silica stones placed in a concrete frame. The pebble construction was first built in 1937, maintained ever since by volunteers, who've now hauled some 20,000 kilos of small white stones up the hill. The visual is arresting. And prideful. Not quite even. But lovely in its obliqueness.

From here I can reach a new stretch of the Kettle Valley Railway, now used mostly by cyclists, and a short distance from Naramata Road I can access McCullough Trestle, one of the KVR's numerous spans. This one is a short straight expanse, a humble trestle with a spectacular view. At this modest elevation I can see down the cut of the gorge across the south of the lake, with Skaha beyond. Along with Penticton. While away to my right, looking north, I can see vineyards that comprise Naramata, the place with the same name as the haughty ship I just left with its sibling. ✿

# THE VIBE
# OF THE PLACE

---

**Driving up the east side** of Okanagan Lake, I'm here to spend time in the village of Naramata. Before arriving, I asked a few people about this part of the valley, the town in particular. And what each person said felt the same.

"Just the vibe of the place. The energy too."

"It's cool. A laid-back energy."

"Near the lake and vineyards. Its history. Cemeteries too. All with their own level of peace."

Perhaps this prepared me in advance, but as I weave the car north on quiet *S*-curves, I feel increasing calm. Gone is the odd traffic aggression from that portion of highway across the water. Maybe road-repair delays fuelled that mad rush. Regardless, this is indeed a new world.

Both sides of the road here are dense with wineries. Now, in the shift of the season, most vines wear a thin drape of insulating mesh. The visual is that of a bedroom in malaria country. Up the road are more vineyards ensconced in netting, the hillside ready for bed, so it seems, tucked in for the night under freshly pressed linens of white.

I ease the car toward the town centre, past a scatter of retail and an inn. It feels like a surf community, and I can see what people were talking about, the relaxed pace of an oceanside destination. No resorts, as such, just the calmness of water, the lake. Somewhat juxtaposed, as this sits at the base of arid hills with the browns of dry pines. And yet, lining the road are verdant vineyards and orchards, desert and fruity oases sharing continuous space.

I park and explore. Streets are numbered, starting at the water. I pass a pub and a pizzeria. Tennis courts in blue concrete. Make my way to the lake, stroll golden beach. The shore is fine gravel, the look of those marmalade cliffs, no doubt the same stone ground into sand. It's almost silent, the only sound a lap of water on shore, a soft wind shushing all around. No upslope or down, simply breeze pulsing over the water. Willow branches and leaves vacillate, the bark the same tone as the beach, which looks like sandpaper, that amber-ish gold. A fine grain for finishing furniture, coarse and yet pleasingly smooth.

I kick off my boots and ease into the lake. The water is cool. Definitely autumn. Bracing. Connecting as well. Away to one side are old pilings, no pier, wood melding with water. Two particularly large

• THE VIBE OF THE PLACE •

willows frame the shore, left and right, like bushy goal posts in yellow and green. Sundogs pierce nimbus, ash blue and grey. While across the lake, the west side, hoodoos brood, the rockface actually scowling. Above that, the ridgeline could be a slim stegosaurus, curved back with clumped trees, mimicking diamonds of bone. A few ribbons of sun light the hills and the water, shimmers like showers, the visual nearly identical. More juxtaposition – sunshine resembling rain – with a slink of ominous, threatening cloud to the south. Time to move on.

From the lake I traipse back through the sand, over gravel, and off to the general store. Everything feels good underfoot, and I'm loath to put boots back on. I could stay here a very long time. That sensation you find somewhere new, invariably on vacation, when you imagine you could move here, live here, and make this new space your home. But a fierce wind snaps me from reverie. A storm is brewing. I pick up my pace, still walking through town, past a sign for *Naramata Regatta*, which is wonderfully fun to say. Equating this place with a surfer town isn't a stretch, as signs advertise SUPs, stand-up paddleboards. No coincidence, I suppose, as this nook of the lake is often glass calm.

The general store is another magical one, selling everything, with the feel of a community centre as well. The only people in a hurry are those from away, passing through. Every local is having a visit, comparing shopping and swapping gossip. I'm reminded of those chatty ravens ahead of the hummingbird reunion. Rushing around here is impossible, so I fall into the groove and browse, find a slab of beef jerky, house made, the best that I've tasted.

Happy and suitably salted, I keep walking along Naramata Beach through Wharf Park as the south wind picks up. A tall mountain ash is heavy with orange berries. More willows. A series of historical photos offer another fresh-air museum, open-page history books, from when the *Naramata* and *Sicamous* trundled through, the bustle of commerce, same as watery railway lines.

This now sleepy village was a cultural centre for settlers, non-Indigenous farmers, ranchers, and tradespeople finding new homes. The lake was the roadway, the big boats shuttling people and goods on the water alongside sailboats, rowboats, and canoes. Regattas have been paramount here for a century, and in the early 1900s this was a hub for live theatre and opera, music and shows. The KVR completed these transport links, connecting this side of the valley to an expanding country-nation that suddenly spanned the continent. The shared bikeway, trail network, and stone oven offer a snapshot of that long, dotted line. Here in Naramata, another intriguing myth lingers, more mixing of European

• THE VIBE OF THE PLACE •

belief with Indigenous legend. The story of how this laid-back wine-growing town took shape.

The area's 20th-century "founder" is considered to be John Moore Robinson, colloquially known as J.M. According to historians, J.M. was deciding on a name for the lake's eastern "fruit ranching" centre, much like he'd done in developing Peachland and Summerland on the opposite shore. One uninspired option was East Summerland, another being New Dominion's Brighton.

But in 1907, having taken a break from building towns faster than he could name them, J.M. attended a séance conducted by the spiritualist Mrs. J.M. Gillespie (their given-name initials being the same is a tidy coincidence). The story goes that in the midst of the séance, Mrs. J.M. informed Mr. J.M. that the late Sioux Chief Big Moose was present in the room, hovering in a corner and relaying his love for his departed spouse, whom he called "Naramatah." And with that, apparently, Mr. J.M. found his new name for the town. Subsequent research indicates Mrs. J.M.'s former spouse had Australian ties, and that the word "Naramata" was thought to be an Aboriginal word meaning "place of water." Either way, the area is now fittingly named.

The plateau that rises behind me, known as the Naramata Bench, was a perennial Syilx camp, used by hunters and gatherers through the Chief

Bitterroot season as spring emerged out of winter. Considered the "house of the bald eagle," it was also a commencement point for Indigenous youth on initiation treks, or rites of passage. An Okanagan vision-quest starting line.

Pondering this under darkening sky, rather than time I've run out of space, exhausting this patch of terrain. I could carry on north, up the east of the lake on rough logging roads, but instead I'll stick to well-travelled tracks, adhere to rental insurance, and keep the car a little less dusty. ✥

# AROUND NARAMATA

---

**I'm spending a good bit of time** around Naramata, the southeast corner of Lake Okanagan, and feel I can indulge any whims that arise, maybe cling to this calm, relaxed vibe. It's penetrated my gait, I've actually been shuffling when walking, and while driving it's all I can do to reach the speed limit, the area shifting things into slow motion. But I have a niggling notion, running like rails and ties. No doubt that long line of boxcars rattling past in Vernon planted the seed. Along with settler history around here, not to mention the KVR trestle with its remarkable view. I need to visit an *actual* railroad station.

Maybe that recent experience near Dairy Queen, the train running through, dredged up this recollection. It was a weeknight. This time of year. Two friends and I walking in town. Not yet driving, so on foot. We were licking our wounds as we'd just been bullied by one, lone bully, which tells you a bit about the bully and a lot about us. So we found our way to a park paralleling the tracks, the CPR that bisects the north Okanagan.

If we had been younger, and cuter, it could pass for an outtake from *Stand by Me* – Stephen King story, Rob Reiner direction. We'd already spent all our coins on the videogame at the 7-Eleven and pushed a shopping cart as far as we could, so it was either create a new diversion or make our way home. Then the song struck our ears. That vibrational hum of a freight train coming our way. And we realized this was our chance to make the evening worthwhile.

We crouched by the tracks as the big train approached, slowing as it rumbled through town at, I would guess, about ten km/h. The horn sounded, that low mournful hoot that begs for black and white film. I don't recall us exchanging a word. Simply knowing what had to be done. The only way to redeem our bruised pride was to jump on that train, ride the rails, destination unknown. Forget school, we'd tie our stuff to a stick and be free. It made perfect sense.

Exchanging a glance and a nod, we committed. Jogged through the dark, sliding on the downslope of gravel, trying to keep pace with the *chug-chug* of steel, a stumbling, aspirational gait. Endless tonnage rolled by, we trotted, then ran, realizing that it was too fast. One friend grabbed a ladder, hoisted up, then another, and I scrambled to do the same thing. Got a hand on a rung, tried to run, then a leap...and I slipped. One of my legs flailed, leaving me certain I was about to lose it. *Unidexter* (a one-legged person) was a word I wouldn't know until later, yet I thought, in that moment, that was my future, as I hung by a hand for a few precarious, terrifying seconds while my free leg dangled beside the crushing grind of the wheels. But with a thrust of adrenaline-fuelled fear I managed to lever myself to the deck of the open-side boxcar, where we rode for ten minutes, enough time for the fresh pee in my jeans to dry. Then we leapt from the train in a scuffle of pitch-soaked ties and sharp rock, felt the welcome relief of skinned knees and wrenched ankles. Every limb still attached.

As the train rumbled on, we howled the maniacal laughs of those who've dodged their demise. At the same instant relinquishing aspirations of riding the rails forever. We even vanquished the assault of the bully, somewhat. Faced down real peril, surviving to retell our tale.

Back in the present, a country song twangs from the radio, I sip cherry juice, a fresh cup in hand, still driving, curious what I'd see if someone had footage of that train-jumping adventure. No doubt quite different from what I recall. And I chuckle as the song playing now has an *actual* railway track, a *musical* track with that unmistakable *chackaboom* rhythm, kickdrum and snare, capturing locomotive and steel.

A meandering drive through orchards and pines gradually pulls me from Naramata. More signage warning of deer, while another states simply:

*bartlett pears, gala apples, and hazelnuts*. No sign of those grumbly clouds from the south, only sun and blue sky. I return to the west side of Okanagan Lake, back to the north-south hum of Highway 97, passing trucks piled with logs, some roughly debarked. A fish shop advertises fresh pickerel. And a café sign states, *Don't Panic, We Have Bannock*, leaving me hungry for bannock.

Rock hills face the lake, vertical tundra, lichen and moss in coppery shades. Quartz stripes on granite, more sandstone. Rosy lines stripe the cliff face in columns and rows, spreadsheets of gemstone and ore. Land fingers probe the lake, deltas of high silty wash, evidence of these bodies of water now shrinking.

There's a cave up a camber of hill, a crack in the slope, maybe home to a troll. Driving once more into Summerland, each embankment feels oddly familiar. Green of trees, brown of earth, arid roll of the land. The same loom of Giant's Head Mountain. Nearby, fake hawks float on orchards, more deterrent to avian thieves. I spot railway signs, ease the car up the west of the valley, slopes littered in toppled trees, upended by wind and erosion. A bright sign points to the Kettle Valley Steam Railway. And I find myself at the end of the road, a dirt car park with rails curving into the forest.

While the CPR connected the north Okanagan with the transcontinental exchange, and steamers and paddle wheelers joined the lake north to south, by the turn of the 20th century a growing immigrant population here in the south of the valley wanted a piece of that action. As ranches and orchards were thriving and silver had been found in the valley, another rail line seemed warranted. Thus, the KVR was envisioned. The line, however, despite its scenic expanse, struggled commercially. Now it's a tourist attraction, a footnote in steel set on wood. Its construction, mind you, same as the CPR, is a patchwork of miserable history. Forced immigrant labour, atrocious conditions. Death in the workplace. An uglier version of mining.

I'm left with an uncomfortable twinge, like entering a museum of human rights, as I park the car and walk to the station. Things are closed and I think that I might be alone, apart from a Clark's nutcracker, feathers dun-black and white, eyeing me from the top of a track junction sign.

But no, two men are here, volunteers, replacing flooring while the facility's closed to the public. I walk to where they are on the platform, learn their names, Bob and Dave, and ask Bob how long he's been here.

"Oh, a hundred years." He grins. "In Summerland."

"How is it?" I ask.

"Okay, not bad. I'm retired, but you gotta keep busy." Another grin. "And I get to play with big toys." He chuckles, then saunters off to the bathroom.

Dave, on the other hand, moved here from Calgary, settling in Peachland.

"Shoulda chosen Summerland," Dave says.

"Why's that?"

"Infrastructure." He thinks about it some more. "Peachland is weird. Maybe too close to West Kelowna. Anyway, I do some consulting now. Oil patch. Volunteer here at the KVR." He squints at the tracks. "They should've left this. The CPR. They've been tearing it up. They left a strip from Penticton up to Summerland but then took out the bridge. Liability. People were jumping off it."

"What, recreational?" I ask. "Or ending their lives?"

"Oh, no. Recreational. Still dangerous though. And these!" He gestures to the showcase locomotive and four passenger cars. "They should be under cover. Not exposed to the elements like this. It's no good. But we had to fight hard just to keep *this*. The railway was fighting the opposite way. Wanting to tear it all up."

Bob, back from the loo, pipes in, "Yeah, worst mistake they ever made. Tearing all that stuff out. Great Northern. Via. All that's left is some Burlington in Vancouver. Out around White Rock." Which is a stretch of track I happen to know from coastal hikes on extensions of the Great Trail.

With smiles and nods, Bob and Dave get back to work, now staining fresh planks on the platform.

The croak of a tree frog echoes from an eave, amplified by the wall and a drain. And I grin, thinking back to my pet frog named Steve, his doppelgänger on Denman Island, and a starring role in my previous Season book.

I make my way up the line, camera in hand.

"Stay off the rails," Bob adds. "They're slippery. That's how you crack a skull."

I let him know I'll be careful.

It's cold as I walk down the rails, and I wish that I'd brought extra layers. Ravens caw as I follow the tracks, disappearing in trees, the visual another time warp, only silent – a mix of melancholy and memory. Maybe the height of the tourist season breathes life into the place. Signs indicate school excursions are offered, with passenger rides, even a gunslinging robbery played out on horseback. All absent right now, leaving me pulling for people like Bob and Dave, hoping these impassioned volunteers are successful. ✿

# A SERIES OF O'S

**A new day.** One more loop of Giant's Head Mountain, like a spaceship slingshotting the moon, and I rocket south to trace these sausage-link lakes to the border. I scoot through Penticton, roughly the same size as Vernon, the two towns framing the big body of water, and follow the west side of Skaha Lake. The highway bears farther west, past Kaleden, where the interestingly named White Lake rests in grass hills. The "lake" is a bone-coloured recess of dry minerals and looks like a place Eddy could've brought camels en route to his pyramids, like a salt path retracing a spice route. Now the road turns gently east, correcting its southerly line to the foot of Skaha, where a series of *O*'s lie ahead: Okanagan Falls, Oliver, and Osoyoos.

The falls of Okanagan Falls have more or less vanished, submerged with the construction of a dam, the waterway now a bare burble, the look of a shallow fish ladder. But the area offers diverse geological colours and shapes. Here the valley creates a narrows, formed as that old glacier carved through Penticton. Rigid land funnelled that flow, an earthy squeeze between outcrops.

Those high hunks of rock are now called Mount McLellan and Peach Cliff. Bighorn sheep make it their home, with mule deer on lower terrain. The land feels more extreme, a shift toward the dramatic. Glacial erratics are here, non-native rock from elsewhere, brought by the movement of ice. The term erratic comes from the Latin *errare*, meaning to roam and to wander, boulders on their very own road trip or quest. One of these is Balancing Rock, a spur to Peach Cliff, supported by granite cobbles. It's reminiscent of a capstone you might see *Looney Tunes*' Road Runner perched on, this one volcanic grey.

Farther south is McIntyre Bluff, a 265-metre-high tatter of white granite, speckled with the same charcoal look as the erratic, the result like a tower of Oreo crumbles. The terrain keeps showing off, technicolour on canvas, with Green Lake away to my right, water loaded with calcium, the same composition as shellfish and pearls. And just beyond that is Mahoney Lake, water blooming with purple bacteria.

I pull in at the next large body of water, Vaseux Lake, and its Migratory Bird Sanctuary. All around, cliffs flex and pose. Eagle Bluff looms, an 800-metre escarpment, in today's light both copper and gold. A lone cricket chirps, amplified like the tree frog and elementary school dove.

When *Kuyeil* was still new I came here to camp and to fish, launching the canoe over rocks in thin weeds. The lake is a continuation of the channel flowing south from Penticton, connecting the valley and finding its eventual way to the sea. Smallmouth bass are found here, tasty and hard to catch. I must've sacrificed six different lures, lost to the rocks and the weeds. Frustratingly fun. If memory serves, I ate bacon, unable to source *mahimahi*.

To the south I see more of that splay-finger sun resembling rain, discombobulating yet oddly affirming. A patchwork of sun hits the water, creating reflecting pools in the midst of the lake. Towering rock protrudes in sharp angles, evident as the sun shifts. Now I see scratches of white on the cliffs. More Nazca lines, maybe, or a petroglyph scrawled by a giant. I'd love it to be a to-do list. 1. *Make list*.

I saunter through sumac along the shoreline, part of this avian throughway. I spot starlings and magpies, more vultures, a bushy lone osprey, and Steller's jays clumped in a band. The jay in particular stands out, the official bird of British Columbia. Vibrant deep blue and black, a sharp comb – often mistaken for blue jays. Part of the intelligent corvid family, same as crows and the magpie that just flitted by, Steller's jays have their own myth. Considered a message of hope in tough times, resilient, these birds are survivors. According to legend these jays are teachers, role models for fearlessness and adaptability. All that's needed to share in this power is to follow their lead.

But rather than empowered, I feel miniscule here by the lake in this towering chasm. When I camped here it felt as though I'd been thrust into the American Four Corners, where Indigenous Anasazi made their homes in sheer cliffs, the sensation one of vastness.

A short hike, some more cherry juice, and I'm back in the car, still heading south on Highway 97. Now into Oliver, where a sign reads, *Canada's Wine Capital*. I stop and admire some vineyards. Grapes in purple and green, none of which I'm familiar with. Things look healthy, despite recent worries around forest fire smoke. Another sharp contrast – verdant crops creep into the hills then stop abruptly, a line of dry brown abutting the green. Clear demarcation of where controlled irrigation begins (or ends). The visual is vibrant. Jarring, yet striking. I could delve into questions around the pumping of water for wine and for golf. Economics. Resource depletion, environmental concerns. I wonder if the Lake Spirit would approve. It leaves the same feeling I had at the trail climbing Giant's Head Mountain: somewhat discouraged, a bit overwhelmed. But rather than saving the world, I jump in the car, turn up the music, and try to retain the Steller's jay lesson. Adaptability, and survival.

On the radio it's another boot-stomping country song, reminding me of a visit I had with a Quebecois man. I was in Montreal for a work event,

• A SEASON IN THE OKANAGAN •

playing hooky, and made my way to Marché Jean-Talon to fashion a picnic and keep hiding. It was there that I met Sylvain, on a pleasant autumn day just like this, mostly sunny and mild.

Sylvain was a busker, playing a beat-up, nylon-string classical guitar. He was seated on an upended apple crate. The crate, the guitar, and the man equally beefy and dusty. Each song concluded with a theatrical "*Merci, merci!*"

I added to Sylvain's upturned hat.

"*Ah, merci! Merci beaucoup,*" he said, "*Je m'appelle Sylvain.*" He extended a meaty hand for a shake, warmly crushing my own, then asked where I was from.

I told him, indicating the top end of Lake Okanagan.

"*Ah, oui,* I spent time in the Okanagan," he said, nodding, then smiling. "Picking fruit." He laughed, an infectious guffaw. "I played a cowboy bar there. In Oliver. *Real cowboys!*"

So of course, that's in my mind as I guide the car into Oliver, dodging cyclists and roadkill while hoping to see *real cowboys*. ❦

( 128 )

Fork in the Road

Apple Orchard,
Summerland

Overleaf:
Fall Harvest,
Peachland

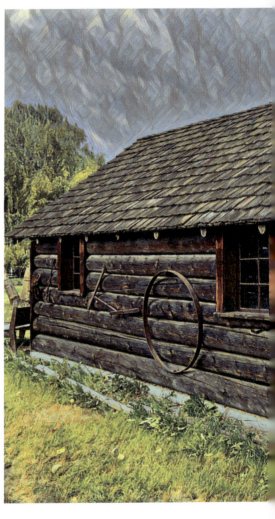

Outbuilding, Pandosy Farm

Charles Pandosy

Pandosy Farmstead

Okanagan Sunflower

Shoreline Pine, Kelowna, with Okanagan Lake Bridge Beyond

# NK'MIP LAND

**Where I am is Nk'Mip land.** The town name Oliver, however, comes from "Honest John" Oliver, premier of BC from 1918 to 1927. A career rancher, Oliver is credited with bringing irrigation to the South Okanagan. Maybe it's that balance of land and resources, the Steller's jay lesson or simply the allure of a narrowing valley, but I'm compelled to delve in, experience desert, and connect, if I can, with the Nk'Mip.

The road undulates to offer a glimpse of Osoyoos Lake, the last big body of water in the valley, stretching across the Canada-USA border. I exit Highway 97 to the Osoyoos Desert Centre. Despite lush irrigation of vineyards and golf courses, most of this valley is perpetually dry, but only *here* is it considered a desert.

The Desert Centre offers a blend of displays, native plant garden, and a long, snaking boardwalk, enabling visitors to get into this arid environment while protecting the delicate plant life and soil. Which I learn is considered semi-arid, a sage and antelope-brush ecosystem. One of the country's most rare, fragile, and endangered ecosystems,

• NK'MIP LAND •

this is home to one of the highest concentrations of at-risk species in Canada: bobcats and burrowing owls, badgers and scorpions. Plus the Great Basin spadefoot, a desert amphibian, as well as a few bears and snakes: racers and gophers and rattlers. None of which I see. Not today, anyway. But I savour the landscape. Like most deserts, it's misleadingly barren yet rich with abundance.

Where I am now is close to Highway 3, the Crowsnest Highway, which I could take east to Castlegar and Creston, or northwest to Keremeos and Princeton, then southwest through E.C. Manning Provincial Park and on to the Fraser Valley. In the same way I was overwhelmed in Naramata with an urge to just stop, settle in, and design a new home, this fork in the road seems to trigger the opposite, a desire to go, fill the tank, and keep driving.

The land, however, has alternate plans. A draw, or near-anchoring effect. Maybe an echo of those wandering erratics; eventually they settle somewhere. I brush dirt from my trousers, return to the car, and carry on to the Nk'Mip Desert Cultural Centre, a space of legend, people, and land. What I find is a quote. "If the very old will remember, the very young will listen." Words from the late Chief Dan George, a man I met, when I was a child, in Vernon. I remember an aura of calm around the Chief. A sensation of wisdom, and reverence. Seeing his words, I feel those same feelings again. A dissolving of time, the shifting of seasons and winds.

I slow the car by a stable where horses are grazing, speckled mustangs and palominos. From here I see the green of the Nk'Mip Canyon Desert Golf Course, along with Nk'Mip Cellars vineyard and winery. And realize that of course balance is attainable. Caring for people, for needs, while ensuring stewardship of the land. I imagine the Lake Spirit nodding as well. Another memory forms, from my stint in those cliffs farther south, past Muriel's home of the Okanogan. Where the Navaho use the word *hózhó*, the balance inherent in all-encompassing beauty. What I'm certain I'm looking at now.

At the Nk'Mip Centre I learn the Syilx word *way'* (pronounced like *white* without the *T* sound). An *aloha*-like word meaning hello and goodbye, another contextual blur and lovely disbanding of time. Inside the state-of-the-art interpretive centre are two mixed-media theatres. Outside is a sculpture gallery and the Living Lands nature exhibit with trails for a walk or a hike. Which I enjoy in strong wind gusting up from the lake, carrying an aroma of sage. The gale swirls, masking direction, and I scramble onto a knoll to spend time with the *Chief*, a sculpture on horseback, created by Virgil "Smoker" Marchand of the Arrow Lakes Band of the Colville Confederated Tribes.

Marchand lived in Washington state, although he did a great deal of work around here. Steel was his preferred art-medium, pieces constructed and bent without heat, simply hammered and viced with brute force. Heat, he explained, would change the steel's natural colour, rob it of beauty. So he fashioned his intricate, outsized sculptures through the most rudimentary of means, bashing great metal slabs into delicate, ethereal pieces. One of which is the *Chief*, which I'm gazing at now, and slowly circling, admiring its fit with the land. The view is of Osoyoos Lake, with the yawn of the valley going north.

The horse-mounted *Chief*, regaled in feather headdress, is hoisting a spear, two-handed, to the sky, palms up, arms open wide. Manifestation and gratitude. Hello and goodbye. All in one gesture. At a glance the sculpture *actually* looks feathered, the steelwork so lifelike, the *Chief* clad in buckskin with tassels, a knife at his side. But everything's metal, colours that match the terrain. The horse, too, is elaborate, sporting feathers and leg bands, desert tones on the metal. In the muscled neck of the mount is the outline of snk'lip, Coyote spiritual guide, howling to the sky. From here I see clouds through the cut of the steel, moving, white over blue, the guide very much alive.

With this powerful image lingering, I get out of the wind, back in the car, and turn south, wanting to see what the border reveals. But what I find first is a finger of land, significant both culturally and geologically. swiẃs Park, a BC Provincial Park managed and operated by the Osoyoos Indian Band. The park has a boardwalk through wetlands, mountain views, and migrating birdlife, a gentler version of Vaseux. But what catches my eye is the long slender spit that stabs out from the west of the lake, almost reaching the opposite shore, a partial land bridge that served travellers on horseback or foot, a natural ford or portage.

Bearing south, I pass orchards with late peaches, new apples and pears, plums splaying in colour and size. The Osoyoos Canal Walkway cuts between beachside motels, where a violent wind whips at the water. Now the Boundary Motel. I've been daydreaming, driving at speed, and realize I'm on top of the border! (Well, a few metres away). I hit the brakes and do a quick U-turn, certain my tire-squeal and about-face must look suspicious. *You there! Halt!* I expect to hear from a bullhorn, accompanied by a warning shot. But no. Everything's quiet. No one around. No doubt I'm not the first to be caught unawares having reached the end of the line.

I park and examine the space, the valley dropping and levelling south. A multi-armed sign points in every direction, tracing cities, the planet, the wind. A large BC flag lunges in northerlies, snapping at Washington state. Along the border, wind howls, dust strafing off hills, the look of ice crystals streaming from Everest. I walk the last stretch of country, the ground underfoot entirely soft, golden sand. I could be on a beach in the tropics. Swallows, meanwhile, swirl in spirograph shapes, indifferent to invisible boundaries. ✿

# DOBRÝ DEN

**Each day I'm aware** of the temperature ratcheting down. If I were to plot daily highs, they'd resemble stairs descending to autumn, Chief Salmon in a split-level walk-down. In the mornings I now need a toque, the ground frosty before sun has risen. Even the winds seem uncertain, waiting to determine direction.

Retracing my route north, I experience the familiar anew. Now, rather than a glacial-valley squeeze I see the corridor open, imagining that vast ice sheet melting, the punchbowl ahead finally thawing. Numbered bridges span creeks around Skaha. A billboard with handprints and footprints says *215, Every Child Matters*. Imagery of small fingers and toes, pressed in flat plaster and painted.

A cottonwood leans on the highway, a canopy under construction. Rivulets veer from Skaha. A floatplane is moored by a beach next to campers. Aging lakeside resorts, more winery signs. A sharp slope of sandy soil. I glimpse the sternwheeler in Penticton, the Naramata Bench. Highway warnings, *EXPECT DELAYS*. Heavy equipment scrapes away hills while propping up others. A worker rappels down a cliff, the rock cinched in gabion wire. The

• DOBRÝ DEN •

road rises, then falls toward water, Okanagan Lake stretching north, where grassy slopes morph into the desert khaki of camouflage.

The sky opens, light cloud in high fluffs. On the ground, sunflowers and vineyards. The temperature eases up, moisture wrung from the air. A sports car tailgates a semi, and I think of a bumper sticker I saw on a fender. *Sorry I'm driving so closely in front of you! #bumperhumpers.*

Southern wineries start to thin while ahead more cluster through Peachland and West Kelowna, grapes changing with latitude. In the south I saw Pinot, Chardonnay, Merlot. Farther north, more Francs and Riesling. When BC's wine scene developed, I remember winemakers from Germany liking conditions in the north of the valley. As the industry grew, more vintners arrived from New Zealand, common climates in new locales.

I stop once again in Summerland, remembering Dave's words at the platform, *Shoulda chosen Summerland*. And I saunter the streets. High school students on lunch break filling fast-food places and convenience stores. I avoid the bustle and find the Sunflower Ukrainian Cafe, where I order and visit with Sasha, asking for a bit of her story.

"I moved from Ukraine six years ago, coming to Canada, to Richmond. Now I've been two months here, in Summerland."

"How's everyone back home?" I ask, afraid of what I might hear.

She shrugs. "Still alive."

I ponder, feelings I don't want to feel. "How's it been here?" I ask, running the gauntlet of trite yet sincere.

"Here, welcoming. Friendly and kind." Her brow furrows. "So many people refer to their Ukrainian roots." She meets my gaze. "Well, because of *now*. And Second World War. And First World War." Another lingering shrug. She smiles. A warm, tired smile.

I have no words. I shrug and smile back, my lunch being prepared in a kitchen behind Sasha. The sound system kicks in, Ukrainian rock gently beating from speakers.

*Dobrý den…Dobrý den…*

Which translates more or less to Hello. A greeting of welcome, and warmth. The song is like an upbeat Oasis tune, or U2's "Beautiful Day." I know it'll loop in my head for a while, but unlike the James Taylor, I don't fight it. Something about it feels proper.

Sasha passes me an exquisite, underpriced meal.

"*Dyakuyu*, Sasha," I say, tapping into visits with Baba and Dido. Thank you.

She smiles. "*Laskavo prosymo*." You're welcome.

Nearly a week goes by, and I return for another midday meal.

The bell on the door jangles as I enter. "*Dobrý den*, Sasha," I say.

### · DOBRÝ DEN ·

"*Pryvit*, Bill," she says with a smile. Hi. Making me not only love this place more, but understand, *truly* understand, what KVR Dave had been talking about.

A bit north I'm surrounded in vistas like the Mary Keith painting from Dan. Fitting, as I'm driving to see him in West Kelowna, to bed down in his living room. A sleepover the same as when we were kids, only now we're not sharing a hide-a-bed, staying up late, and giggling. Now we giggle and go to bed early. Sports on TV, a platter of barbeque, sunset on mountains. Next morning I'm told that my snoring is stupendous. I inform Dan it's his cooking.

To which Dan shares a story of my dad and fried bacon. Something that Dad preferred *burned*.

"So, you want it crisp?" every server would say.

"No," Dad would clarify, using the tone he'd use for a disobedient pet. "*BURNED*." As he did, in fact, like his bacon charred black. Something no cook wants to send from their kitchen. And so Dad would invariably be served crisp bacon, which was not what he wanted, nor asked for. And he'd sigh. Eat his crisp bacon. And hope that next time they might get it right.

For the next few days I deplete Danny's fridge, then carry on to Kelowna, to the home of my brother Norm, feeling I'm getting quite good at freeloading. Norm came into my life when I was a child. The same season I first woke to the mourning dove. My parents had three children – my two sisters and me, but Norm is my brother. One of those treasured nonfamilial relations you choose.

You may know Norm from that season on Vancouver Island, when I shared the story of a hawthorn that supported a swinging basket-style chair at our home. Norm was the unlucky swinger (so to speak) who happened to be in the seat when the frayed piece of rope that held it in place finally snapped, sending Norm tumbling down the slope of the yard in the cage-like contraption, giving my brother a wicker-wrapped dunk in the lake while the rest of us looked on, as though witnessing a well-choreographed stunt. Fortunately, Norm was all right, the chair decommissioned. But of course, I believe in that moment Norm invented the adrenaline-fuelled pastime of zorbing.

I make Norm's home my own for a while, loving the space and its owner. A shared Ukrainian heritage ensures what he cooks is superb, and abundant. And in the same way I felt the Lake Spirit was there with the *Chief* on the Nk'Mip knoll, here I feel certain that Baba and Dido are not only watching but smiling. ❖

# **CULTURAL DISTRICT**

---

**Sun rises in leisurely rose,** hanging first on the horizon, before brightening to pink. Over breakfast I ask Norm about Kelowna, as he's lived here for two decades.

"It's grown a lot. A far cry from what it was when I came here." Offering diverse amenities, while still compact in size. "Nothing like that now, though," he adds, reflecting on growth and its residue. "We'll just have to wait and see."

A morning hug and he heads off to work while I drive to downtown Kelowna, leave the car, and continue on foot. I stroll sidewalks and grass until I get to the water, roughly the middle of Lake Okanagan. Where a high, slender sculpture stands by the marina, white fibreglass called *Spirit of Sail*, by Robert Dow Reid. A stylized depiction of wind-filled sails, perspective from the bow or stern of a ketch, mid-jaunt, as though the craft's gusting out to the lake. If I had to guess I'd say the *Spirit of Sail* is catching a warm Zephyrus, those westerly winds aligned with the water.

From the marina I hear the *ping* and *ting* of metal rigging on masts, a few yawls with the yachts. Wind picks up, raising the pitch to near-whistling sounds. And I think of the music associated with boats and with oars, the cadence of singing consistent with rowing and paddling, keeping tempo, raising spirits, passing time. Although singing is common, I know of Indigenous paddlers who refuse to whistle when out on the water, as legend states whistles call winds. Winds that bring ill-tempered waves that flip boats. And I think of the blustery god Eurus, unhoused, frustrated, justifiably angry.

A lakeside walkway curves down the shore, brackets the marina. I keep strolling, grab a coffee, admire the lake. Shoreline with rushes in yellow-topped snowberry, plants growing wild. A number of walkers, locals and tourists. Mallards paddle the shallows and fingerlings speckle the surface in rings. A duck-bum points up, its owner munching on milfoil.

A handful of people lounge on the grass, soaking up the sun. I hear a small stereo set on a towel. Bob Marley, "One Love." It turns out today is World Gratitude Day, the sentiment apropos. A rollerblader skates by in wave curls and curves. A parasail glides in bright yellow, hauled by a blue and white speedboat. The boat throttles down, the parasailer descends, gets a dunk, then the boat speeds away, yanking the trailing passenger skyward.

From the walkway I cross grass, then sand, to a pier where an angler is baiting his line, the view a mixture of water and hills, a resort and casino beyond. I creak down the pier and strike up conversation. The fisherman's name is Jeff.

"Whatcha fishing for?" I ask Jeff.

"Trout."

"Anything?"

"Nah," Jeff shakes his head. "But a guy, just the other day, got a two-pound rainbow trout outta here."

"That's a meal."

"Sure is. Just nice to get a line in the water."

I nod in agreement.

Jeff gives my hand a good shake, then adds, "You have a good day now, ya hear?"

As I walk up the pier, the blue and white speedboat goes by. No sign of the parachute. I can't help but wonder if the dangling tourist is still airborne, untethered, now drifting away down the lake toward Eddy's Kingdom.

Back on land, in the park, on a flat of red brick, is a likeness of Ogopogo snaking its way through some greenery, a sculpture from 1960 created by Peter Soelin. Nothing like the Lake Spirit, this monster is pure Euro-settler legend with a touristic bent. A serpent's body undulating like whitecaps, scales and stegosaur fins, with a head like a giraffe, topped with two knobby protrusions, which I learn are called ossicones. The statue looks freshly painted. A cream-coloured belly, green sides, a brown razor-back top. And an open-mouthed smile, red tongue lolling, as though blowing a raspberry.

By the visitor centre I chat with another Dave, who stands at a bit of an angle with the aid of a bright copper cane.

"How long you been here?" I ask.

"Thirty years," Dave replies. "Well, 29."

"You like it?"

"Love it!" he beams. "I taught skiing, and golf. Before I got sick. Twelve years. Got paid well. Some of the best skiing in the world. Some of the best golf too. I came here from up north."

"Where abouts?"

"Peace Country. Fort St. John, Dawson Creek, Chetwynd. Made enough money to get out of there. Come down here. Had *enough* of that 40 below. *No thanks!* Not anymore. Been here ever since." Dave's eyes twinkle as he smiles, his love of the place infectious.

With smiles and waves I move on, where I find another tall statue. This one simply called *Bear*. Made of steel, *Bear* was built in 2010 by artist Brower Hatcher. Its inspiration is the fact that "Kelowna" is an anglicized translation of the Syilx word *kiʔlawnaʔ*, meaning grizzly bear. The statue's light in design although massive, a tribute to the lake and the city.

• CULTURAL DISTRICT •

The beast sits atop a high plinth and captures the sky with each view. Steel joints glint in the sun and I can't help but see constellations – Ursa Major and Minor – maybe relations to this very kiʔlawnaʔ.

From the sweep of the beach and treed park, I backtrack through Kelowna's downtown. Tidy trimmed lawns surround City Hall, planted with palms, a tropical feel in the arid brown valley. A sparrow flits to a tall purple willow. Someone sleeps in the shrubs, a green and blue sleeping bag wedged amongst roots. I carry on through the Cultural District, an array of museums like scattered snapshots, fanning perspectives. To the city bus exchange, where a community of unhoused locals socialize, belongings in small piles and in shopping carts. There's laughter and sharing. Thick leafy trees throw some shade on the sidewalk, rain cover too, I presume. The feel of established residency.

From Water Street I walk though a roundabout to Kasugai Gardens, a manicured pocket of park created to acknowledge the connection with Kasugai, Japan, sister city to Kelowna. The garden is a quiet green gem, a near-silent space tucked in the bustle. Birdsong is vibrant, muting the surrounding downtown. In a curved central pond I see koi in white, black, and orange. Halloween colours, languidly swimming, occasionally breaking the surface. Another memory of the house by the lake, where we'd see on occasion, for a great many years, two monstrous goldfish. Ten kilos each, at least. Leaving us to question their provenance. Goldfish released in the wild? An Okanagan version of flushed baby alligators? Or simply two koi set free, someone having moved or filled in their pond.

Dragging myself from the calm of the garden, I cut through a hedge of lavender sage, busy with buzzing bees, to access Okanagan Heritage Museum, where I'm flung once again into history. One of the most in-depth and representative exhibitions I've seen.

The first image that grabs me is the museum logo. A handprint imposed on a grizzly bear paw, white on red. Like an ancient cave painting, human palm in red ochre, only this one is set in the track of the city's namesake, an earthly Ursa overlooking the lake.

I follow arrows, a gentle loop to the left, pulling me through eons. More imagery of calendar pages, seasons ratcheting past. I see depictions of the coast pushing in, mountains forming, blasting volcanoes, all of it smothered in ice. Next to black and white drawings are actual pieces of rock: granite, gneiss, and basalt. A plaque states, "The Okanagan Valley is one of BC's largest earth structures." Nearly 200 million years of geological activity.

I try to perceive, put it in context, but give up and move on to the animals. A few fossils. Bison bones.

• CULTURAL DISTRICT •

The snout of an ichthyosaur, a massive marine reptile from the Parnassian Sea, a body of water that, according to the museum, covered this valley. If I wanted to find a link with that giraffe-headed serpent sticking out its tongue in the park, this ancient beast could be it. I wish I could ask Susan Allison, the settler who saw the dinosaur in the lake. Maybe *this* was what she had seen.

Next to this is a landscape display of current wildlife, now taxidermied and staring, glass-eyed. On a mound is a coyote, a flesh-and-bone snk'lip, teacher of natural laws. Taking me back to a night on my own in the hills south of Vernon, tucked in a cottage, a small house in a groomed stretch of wild. This time of year. Early sunset. And I was grilling a steak for my supper. Playing with my food, experimenting with charcoal, a blend of three hardwoods. When the coals were ready, glowing orange, I made a nest of moist rosemary stalks, which smoked and then charred as my steak hit the heat. The result, meat infused with both smoke and rosemary. Simple, effective, delicious.

As I cut into my meal, from across a small dip in the land coyotes howled, a chorus of yips and yelps, punctuated by long and lingering yowls. Chilling. Evocative too. Hackles rose on my neck, but I wasn't afraid. Just aware of being part of the land. A sensation once more of being an environ-organism, a visit from distant cousins. Watchers and teachers, these ones part of a pack. I sat. I listened. Another dissolving of time. Only now do I realize one of that choir might have been snk'lip, ushering in a new season.

From the faux hill with the museum coyote, I move to the next exhibit. A recreated pit house, much like a kekuli from the cirque overlooking Kal Lake. An ingenious display, constructed for the museum by Syilx Elder Eric Mitchell, an authentic winter home, a qʷćiʔ, but built in a one-quarter design, cleverly set with angled mirrors to create the visual appearance of a complete, circular dwelling. A bit like that James Bond film, where you know the villain is in the mirrored room, but are unsure which image is a reflection and which one is real. Only here it's just me. Good guy and bad. Now rubbing his (my) head as I've clocked it on a low-hanging beam. Four, in fact, if you count our reflections.

I sit in the space for a while, imagining winter in here, through a season of Chief Black Bear. Boreas huffing outside. Bannock, perhaps, on the fire. A small sign shares the Seven Teachings: *Love, Humility, Respect, Truth, Honesty, Wisdom, Bravery*. Whether the space or the words I'm uncertain, all I know is I'm humbled.

The structure is bark-free timber, stout logs bound like carvel-built ships. A single notched log protrudes through the ceiling and roof, a ladder that leads to an opening that would serve as an entryway, smoke hole and watch post. A bench wraps around the interior, space for sitting and working, sleeping and eating, the space cozy, inviting, secure. A low entryway faces east. The design, facing sunrise, is something I've seen everywhere. Shelters and homes, places of worship and burial plots. Irrespective of faith or religion, something about the alignment crosses all boundaries, every culture and every locale. Which I find reassuring. Global commonality.

The notched ladder leans at a steep angle, the look of a slanted totem. Part of the design would serve as defense, intruders less likely to navigate the descent with confidence, an effective deterrent to burglars. Elder Mitchell explains that navigating the ladder pole not only protects the home, but builds confidence in young residents, helping them overcome fears.

Circling displays, I come to flora and fauna, exhibits of wetland and grassland, aquatic, subalpine, and forest. The rare creatures I "saw" in the desert next to long-legged waders and fierce raptors. A muskrat, a beaver. A goose and a grebe. Fist-sized mussels and clams. With big game as well: mountain goats, black bears and cougars. All of it found around here. With a flourishing finale there's an example of everything, clustered in a single display, almost biblical, half an ark's worth of creatures towering to the ceiling.

Next I see settler history. A cabin, snowshoes, a rifle, traps, and plush furs. A timeline plotting the arrival of Europeans. With an expansive exhibit of the Four Food Chiefs, guiding through seasons. Along with descriptions and videos are high-hanging paintings, depicting each season and Chief. Colours of transition, warming and cooling, cooling and warming, thrusting me back through the valley, eras of water and wind. All of it happening now.

I conclude with the richest display yet, speaking to what I encountered while getting here, the community out front with no address, still a place of defined belonging. There's an artistic graph, a pie chart, that could pass for a wildlife track, the print of a multi-clawed foot. *Reasons for Homelessness in Kelowna*. The footprint graph is dominated by high cost of living, lack of safe housing options, family conflict. These are well over half of the *Reasons*. Addiction a mere 10 per cent of the chart.

I keep reading. *What does homelessness look like in Kelowna?* "Many people experiencing homelessness in Kelowna describe feeling excluded from the larger community. They also tell stories of resilience, resourcefulness, and friendship. In the midst of these shared experiences, each person has their own story."

There's a photo of a woman named Georgia, an open face looking straight at the camera, next to her quote, "I don't even feel comfortable going into a restaurant to have a meal, going out on a date with my husband, because I get looked at like I don't belong there. It doesn't matter how well I dress, how well I look, because they know me from the street."

Next, a shot of a man named Chris, sporting a shy grin. "There's a lot of people down there [on Leon Avenue] that aren't down there because they want to be, that's for sure."

And a large photo of a woman named Laurie, its title, *SEE me*. Laurie's quote, "You're always accepted here no matter what. They leave you alone here. Right now, I can sit down and you're not at risk of really anything major. Here on Leon, compared to the rest of the city. Why do I come here? Why do people come here? That's why. Not judged. Not gawked at. I just feel normal."

Next to the pictures is a slightly bent crutch, hospital issue, a shopping cart and tarpaulin. No wonder I felt so at ease out front, past the busses and down Leon Avenue. This is a place of belonging. Acceptance. Along with commitments for aid and for change. I spend extra time contemplating perspectives. Unlike multimillion-year timespans, this is easy to grasp. Impossible not to relate.

Completing the museum loop, I feel like I've surfaced from a depth, rising through water, informed and exhausted. But before I return to the street,

I meet with a curator. Elizabeth. It's quiet and she welcomes the visit.

"How long have you been here?" I ask.

"Forever!" she laughs, although she's not old. Maybe 30 years is forever.

"And how is it?"

"Oh, the changes. So much. Even the past five years."

"How so?"

She gestures behind me, indicating all around, ten-storey buildings surrounding the museum. "The tall buildings," she says. "The skyline. It's just gotten so much bigger." She pauses. Thinks about it. "But I like it. And I love working here."

The space certainly has a good energy. An inside version of Naramata, to a degree. A good fit to what I witnessed out front, in the quotes and the photos. Reminders of Steller's jay lessons. Hope in tough times. Resiliency, adaptability. Survival. ♣

# THE MISSION AND FATHER PANDOSY

---

**From the museum** I return to the car and go across town. A roll of low hills, the lake a short distance away. Buildings shrink, thinning to orchards and agriculture. I drive south to Okanagan Mission, now a neighbourhood in greater Kelowna. Also known as simply the Mission, this part of the valley, this side of the lake, is named for Father Charles Pandosy, considered the founder of a European-settled Kelowna.

"It is a great valley situated on the bank of the great Lake Okanagan. All who know it praise it. The cultivable land is immense," wrote Pandosy upon arriving here in the late 1850s, his task to open a mission. He came to the valley with Father Richard and Brother Surel, the three men OMI, or Oblates Mary Immaculate.

Along with a few settlers, the OMI spent their first winter just north of here, near the beach where the *Four Food Chiefs* statue now stands on Pelmewash Parkway. In 1860, the small group moved south along Syilx land to where the Rivière de l'Anse au Sable, or Mission Creek, cuts through grass fields

( 165 )

into Lake Okanagan. They named the locale Mission de l'Immaculée Conception, their farmstead becoming a thriving agricultural and ranching enterprise, as well as a community hub for Syilx and settlers.

The creek, bordered in poplars and cottonwoods, was always a meeting place for the Syilx, a market of sorts, where Black Mountain flint was gathered from hills and brought here for knapping, shaped into tools for cutting and scraping, turned into arrowheads, spear points, and knives. It was also a prime fishing spot, accessible and abundant with salmon and trout.

Parking at the Father Pandosy Mission, now an open-air museum, I'm steeled for what I might find, knowing that many OMI missionaries were part of Canada's residential school horrors. But what greets me in the centre of the acreage is a statue of Pandosy, an infusion of Syilx imagery by Indigenous sculptor Crystal Przybille. The sculpture is two metres high, the same height as the man, and folds Okanagan culture into the priest's lifelike depiction, striding with purpose in a southerly gust.

Circling the sculpture, I feel I can glean a sense of Pandosy in conjunction with the land and its culture. In the flow of his clerical robes are reliefs of the Food Chiefs: Bitterroot, Saskatoon, Salmon, and Bear, with snk'lip winding through all of it. According to Przybille, the work is here to heighten awareness of Syilx culture, and the impact of settlers and settlement.

• THE MISSION AND FATHER PANDOSY •

"The sculpture is intended to stand for generations to publicly inspire awareness and contemplation regarding Okanagan Valley history, both of Euro-Canadian and Okanagan First Nation/Syilx. It will enhance a sense of local identity and encourage us to consider how circumstances in our valley came to be so."

Making my way around the farmstead, I enter outbuildings and homes. It was here the original settlers, along with Pandosy, cultivated the first apples and grapes in the valley, starting two prodigious industries, as well as raising cattle and horses. Many of the 19th-century buildings still stand, some having been moved from nearby to create a cross-section of settler community. Physically I'm alone, the entire space to myself. But from one of the old structures a smoke alarm's dying, a low battery beeping a single-note warble, somehow unravelling time.

I complete a full circuit, drawn again to the Pandosy statue. The Food Chiefs, the Coyote, the priest's chiselled visage, determined and stern. Awareness, I wonder, of something unfound in his sermons? Despite the carved robes in gusts, today there's an absence of wind, gods and seasons withholding opinion. In Pandosy's hand a forked branch is clenched, his robes a curtain of contour with a thick leather belt, all together resembling a tree. The look of old growth returning to the land. And it was

• A SEASON IN THE OKANAGAN •

here archaeologists found the priest's unmarked grave, unearthed in the 1980s – Pandosy buried in his prized vegetable patch, his rosary and cross discarded. ✤

Predator Ridge, Vernon

Ripe for the Picking

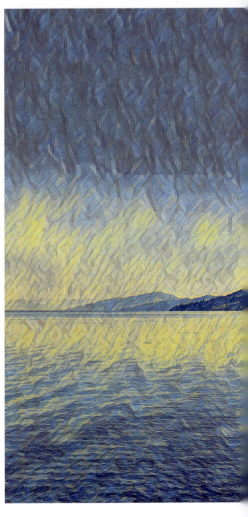

Paul's Tomb, Okanagan Lake

Okanagan Lake, Looking South

Chipmunk, Knox Mountain

Overleaf:
New-Growth Pine

Ponderosa in Cloud

# SNCƏWIPS

---

**A few days pass** and I head south again, crossing the Okanagan Lake Bridge into hills around West Kelowna. I'm going to Sncəwips Heritage Museum of the Westbank First Nation for a visit with Sadie, one of the friendly, informative curators. The building, its contents, and the land that it sits on remain a protected cultural space. Heritage shared in rich art, with oral stories of the Syilx from a sqilx$^w$ perspective.

At the moment a film's being made. I stand back and watch as a group squeezes in frame. Filming seems to be focused on the central exhibit, a spectacular wooden canoe. Unlike the ribbed birchbark variety, this vessel looks solid, or at the very least, heavy. Bentwood lashed in thick bands. It resembles something I'd expect to see on the Amazon, like a hollowed-out totem or phone pole. I can't imagine portaging. But it's beautiful. Blond timber with charcoal grains.

Around the rest of the room are bundles of wicker and reeds, the kind used for building and shelter. I'm reminded of Sveva Caetani's bold paintings hanging from walls. All this next to beaded leather and gloves, tasselled moccasins, stone adzes and arrowheads, with a heavy gourd urn, intricately painted with feather and floral designs. It almost looks Japanese, the flat art I'd expect to see with backdrops of Fuji or cherries in blossom. On another wall stands a fishnet, handheld on a pole, design unchanged for millennia, next to the multi-point rack of a stag.

I don't stay long but return a while later, hoping to learn more. Sadie's still here, filming still going on. I watch the crew work. I shift my focus to the museum logo, a circular Lake Spirit, or Ogopogo. Its branching tail could be mycorrhizal roots, dorsal fins in small waves, resembling Steller's jay eyes. With a long row of spots on its side, like portholes, leaving us to wonder who's looking outward, or in.

From Sadie I learn more about Ogopogo, the *actual* legend, from long before settlers arrived. From the Syilx perspective, the name of the Spirit is n'x̌ax̌aitkʷ (pronounced n-ha-ha-it-koo), the sacred entity that protects the water and valley. Many are still certain the Spirit resides at the bend in the lake under Rattlesnake Island. But the legend goes deeper, to the symbiosis of ecosystems, people and land, the lake itself being vital. The imperativeness of maintaining clean water, balancing harvests with preservation.

The lake *monster* notion arose from those early settlers, stories of stolen horses and dinosaurs. And the ignorance that confused Indigenous gratitude gifts with sacrifice, considered idolatry and condemned by obstinate clergy. Over time, zealous marketers couldn't resist glomming onto settler stories of monsters and mystery, the potential tourist-draw too alluring to not exploit. Which sowed most of the tales I grew up with, the belief that maybe gargantuan sturgeon were there, waiting to swallow small children. Or it could've been a venerable plesiosaur, similar to yeti and sasquatch. Not the creatures themselves but the same twist of legend. When storytelling no longer perpetuates culture but instead becomes a warped game of pass-it-on.

I suspect I'm once again in the way of the film crew, so I retreat to the next room with Sadie, who coaches me, bumbling, through pronunciation of a few Syilx words in nsyilxcən. Part of Salish linguistics, here the language is distinct from neighbouring Nations. Undulating dialects that resemble topography.

Smiling and patient, Sadie helps me practice new phrases. Which we're now doing softly, aware of the filming in the adjacent room. I can't help but smile, reminded of high school band, when our teacher wanted us to play at a whisper, the term *sotto voce*. Which we never quite mastered, resulting in our teacher's frustration and inevitable yelling.

"*Sotto voce!*" he'd scream. "*Sotto voce!*"

• SNCəWIPS •

Which of course we assumed meant LOUDER, so we'd blast on our horns until the bell finally rang and we'd leave, all believing we'd done rather well.

Sadie, mind you, is an excellent teacher, our volume just right, as she shares another recap. *nsyilxcən is the language. Syilx, the people. sqilx$^w$, the Indigenous perspective.* Precisely what this museum is here to communicate. Broadly speaking, the Okanagan.

After the lesson, I'm convinced that I did fairly well. Mind you, I thought the same leaving band class. The few words Sadie's taught me are still a challenge for me to say, never mind trying to write them. One of the reasons early transcribers came up with Latinate transliteration – academics and translators designing their own written language, a kind of Rosetta Stone for scholars. But for those of us ignorant of the embouchure shapes and throat sounds of unfamiliar language, the words can at times be as puzzling as someone shouting when they want quiet.

The filming continues and I run through my short list of words once again. Take a lingering look at displays. Heritage. History. Then I thank Sadie and make for the door. But she stops me and calls me back. To gift me with a bundle of sage, tied in soft cloth in a sunflower shade, drawn with a fine yellow thread. What's inside my small satchel is called q$^w$əlq$^w$əlmniłp, or big sagebrush. Known for its medicinal properties, this gesture of friendship and gratitude can also accompany the sharing of food. Traditionally it might be offered when travelling, meeting new people, or gifting to the spirits of water and land.

I'm touched, feeling instantly blessed. Much more than the healing nature inherent in sage, more than a few spoken words, even more than the showcase of culture found here. I sense a strengthened connection to the valley itself. A place I knew as my home but now deepened. Enhanced in a manner a conductor might call *fortissimo*, when the volume of something can be overwhelming. Surrounded in something unseen, but heard, and felt, vibrationally. An earth tremor. And I can't help but wonder which direction the wind's blowing now.

I drive for a while. Quiet, reflective. I pull over and take a few photos. Colours somehow enhanced, as though through a filter. Some cloud overhead, ivory-grey, an unsettled mix hints at rain. While traffic hums by I take out my bundle of sage and pinch the bag to release the aroma. There's the rich familiarity of kitchen herbs, what I associate with roast dinner on special occasions. Usually a whole chicken, skin on. But again, there's something much more. Earthiness. Savoury. If my nose could distinguish umami, this would be it. Gardens in autumn. Squashes and beans. A pumpkin as well. Then it hits me. This is the scent of the season. Time of Chief Salmon, Notus, and southern fall air.

It triggers a memory of another deep lake in the hills at the valley's north edge where, years ago, a grave was dug in the shore. For the burial of Interior Salish Chief Pinaus. As a boy, I'd ride my bike by the water and gravesite, a bike the same red as *Kuyeil*. Over ensuing seasons, the shoreline crumbled to reveal the Chief's tomb, his bones the colour of ivory. Despite having lost both my uncles, those plots near Baba and Dido, it was my first tactile encounter with death. Gritty. Muddling afterlife with erosion, things bathed in new light. Not to mention the timeline of seasons and land. ✿

# LAKE MUSIC AND ASH

---

**An alarm wakes me** ahead of the sun. In fact it'll be dark for a while. Cold too. Close to freezing. I pull on more layers and drive up the east edge of the big lake, in the loom of Knox Mountain, one of those ancient volcanoes. I'm starting the day with a hike and a visit with Michael, a good friend I met a few years ago. Musician, songwriter, and producer, Michael not only mentored my music, building on my tutelage from Summerland, but recorded and engineered my own indie album as well.

From his lakeside home he greets me with a warm smile and embrace, both of us bundled in jackets and toques, a slim travel guitar also slung on his shoulder. And we head out for a climb, a gradual ascent that loops along the side of the mountain. At our feet, cliffs drop to the water, Okanagan Lake yawning, now warming in fall tones, sunrise shades of maple red gold.

We amble and climb for a while, undulate and descend, birdsong and lake our companions, until we come to a place called Paul's Tomb, named for settlers Rembler and Elizabeth Paul. The Pauls built one of the very first settler cottages here, overlooking the lake. Rembler, a veterinary surgeon, may be best known for his passion and caring for animals. The lakeside tomb was constructed as a family plot, sufficient to accommodate a few generations of Pauls.

Today it's as peaceful as when I visited the cemetery in Vernon. Only colder. Settling on a log on the beach, Michael unslings his guitar, tunes it, passes it to me.

"Whatcha been writing?" he asks with a smile.

I blow into my hands, get some feeling in fingers, and play.

Michael laughs as I sing, the lyrics sounding made up. But no, fortunately I do have something fresh to share, and as the song unfolds I manage to remember most of it.

I pass the guitar back and Michael plays a song of his father's, one of many songs his dad wrote, which Michael learned, then recorded, after his father had passed. Each original tune provided an unfiltered look at the man and the artist, beyond simply being his father. Singing by the water we remember our dads, share a silent cry, then climb the hill and go home.

Another week eases by and I'm returning to Vernon, driving north from Kelowna, the road wedged between lakes. Through Lake Country, past the *Four Food Chiefs* and Kal Lake, the road offers an elevated look at the top of the valley, its thick glacial track carved behind me.

I'm here to visit my mom, and to celebrate her ninetieth birthday. The venue she's chosen has us lunching in sun on a patio, a pub at the end of Okanagan Lake's thumb. Up a hill is a tree farm, a ranch. Across the water are houses, a golf course, an orchard. Beyond that, our old lot, the ponderosa still standing guard.

Over a burger and shrimp we share photos and laugh. Reminisce. A good lunch and an excellent visit. Then something I hadn't expected – I'm given Dad's ashes. It's been a few years since he died, and I thought I had said my goodbyes. Only now I'll revisit it all. Another conclusion, perhaps.

I take Mom to her mid-rise apartment, meet her neighbours and friends. More laughter and hugs. Then she sends me off with a few homemade cookies. Butterscotch. Which I'm sure will pair well with the last of my cherry juice.

I say farewell to family and friends, and I'll now make my way to the airport just north of Kelowna. Drop the rental car too, which I'll miss. Sensors, plush seats, lofty views. Space for cookies and coffee, and juice. But before that, I've one final stop.

Taking time, I take it all in. Lake and hills.

No hummingbirds, yet, on this trip. Though I know they still make this their home.

• LAKE MUSIC AND ASH •

I park the car, grab water and snacks, and scramble into the hills. Where pine needles blanket the ground over pink and orange rock, with cacti and clumps of wild grass. A crow caws as a magpie swoops by. Above that, cirrus in ribbons on blue. Finally I stop climbing, resting in evergreen shade, next to a saskatoon berry tree. My seat is the ground, pine cones and dirt. And I break out my picnic, cookies and water. With a lingering guzzle of cherry juice.

It's warm in the sun, even now in residual autumn. No wind. The lake calm, far below. And I take out Dad's ashes. Remember his bench in town. *Loved by the town that he loved.* From here we can see the valley stretch out, the big lake, even make out the old ponderosa, watching it all from a height. We had picnics here too. Dad and me. Through each of the region's four seasons.

The small packet resembles my sage bundle from Sadie. Its own gift of caring, of thanks. I unwrap the ashes, remember, and smile. Then I let Dad return to the land, this place that he treasured, passing on a shared love. To my amazement a light breeze arrives, perfect swirls, a spindle in every direction. Ashes whoosh in a tiny tornado, spin for a moment, then fly. ✿

# CONCLUSION

*A New Gust of Breeze*

Jammed in another small plane, this one bearing southwest, ahead of a gusting new season. I sense a rumble from Chief Black Bear, ready to take charge from Chief Salmon. Wind shifting as well, Notus to Boreas, bringing a northerly bite. Time to get back to my home by the sea, settled on Coast Salish land, a meld of seawater that connects with the lakes that I followed, up and down through the curve of the valley. An echo of snk'lip, along with Ogopogo, Lake Spirit.

I think of that flow, glacial melt, now the lakes with their rivers, canals. As though reinventing. And yet that's not accurate, because just like the seasons, everything finds a new iteration. Like the alder wood slice and the trim of *Kuyeil*. Dad's ashes as well. That last swirl of calcium dust, seemingly circling the spot where I sat. View of valley, the lake, the lone ponderosa. Another calendar page being flipped with a new burst of breeze. One more season to find our way home. ✤

# A NOTE ABOUT NAMES AND NARRATION

**To the best of my ability** I've shared regional names, places and people, in phonetic translations of Indigenous language. Even in working with patient experts like Muriel and Sadie, research reveals different spellings, alternate meanings, varying interpretation. While my own heritage is from settlers who moved for opportunity, safety, and to make a new home, I want to convey my deep appreciation of the First Peoples who live on this land. That continuity of culture and stewardship furthers my ongoing gratitude and passion for this place and its people. Along with a handful of learned words, what I may recall best is Sadie's overview, a reminder of the Okanagan region and its people. *nsyilxcən is the language. Syilx, the people. sqilx$^w$, the Indigenous perspective.*

In writing each Season book, my concern is the risk of imparting a settler's perspective onto inherently regional narratives. While acutely aware of this, I persevere, hoping that sincerity speaks to what we all feel, something I've noted previously with respect to writing travel memoirs. Beyond spelling and pronunciation, some words can be subjective. Many immigrants put their own labels on places, or retained Indigenous names but phonetically adapted them into formats consistent with other languages. The result is a form of transliteration in which spoken words are effectively reinvented, changed into newly written formats. Oftentimes, how best to say and to use these reinvented names is only familiar to those who speak the original tongue, translators, or scholars versed in regional narratives. According to the Government of Canada, "Each jurisdiction's approach is different, reflecting its particular geography, history and circumstances." With respect to place names in particular, the government adds, "This long-term work is still evolving as a means of representing the coexistence of all the cultures that have built our past and our present history."

In my previous Season book I shared an island vignette from Hawaii, taken from the lava fields of Big Island. It's a place where locals lay pieces of white coral on the cocoa-hued ground, spelling out words of compassion: ALOHA, LOVE, HOPE. Words are visually bold, the distinction of light over dark. But more than the contrast of colour, what's striking is the fields of old rock came about from past violence, eruptions of magma and stone, now grown into land where sentiments of caring prevail. Another time blur, shift of season, and transition toward

• A NOTE ABOUT NAMES AND NARRATION •

something better. In effect, a stone installation much like Crystal Przybille's commanding sculpture of Charles Pandosy, blending Syilx imagery with a Euro-settler figurehead. Finding commonality, melding narrative and culture in communal space, recognizing the fact that *all* space is shared. ❖

# ACKNOWLEDGEMENTS

**Writing a travel memoir** is a personal endeavour, but creating a book is a team effort. And for that hardworking team I'm most grateful. At RMB | Rocky Mountain Books our team includes publisher Don Gorman, with the marketing efforts of Grace Gorman and James Faccinto. Editing and proofing make a book readable, and for that I have Kirsten Craven, Kelly Laycock, and Peter Enman to thank. And with a book of this nature, design expertise makes it beautiful. For this I thank Lara Minja.

The artwork you see is my own, photos I take and then digitally paint, but I purchased the two initial map outlines before styling, adding details, and then having Lara make them better. Credit for the outline of BC goes to iStock and Ruslan Maiborodin, while credit for the outline of Lake Okanagan goes to Design Bundles.

Family and friends clearly played an integral role in this excursion. Thanks to Norm, and to Dan. Michael too. With love and thanks to my mom, and to those I was able to visit at that time. My sister Bobbie, my nieces Melissa and Christy. And the wonderful people I met, many of whom are now friends. Thanks to Doug, to Ginger, and Brian, whose name I changed for discretion. To Melinda and Sasha, David, Bob and Dave, as well as Ally, Aeris, and Elizabeth.

Thanks once again to Sadie and Muriel, two cultural experts who have consistently given their time to make the world better. With additional thanks to each reader, book lender, seller, and buyer. Your support makes this possible. Please know that you are contributing to the well-being of many people. And it's greatly appreciated.

Of course all my love goes to Deb, who encourages and supports my pursuits, raising my bar and catching me each time I fall. I can't thank you enough.

# ABOUT THE AUTHOR

**Bill Arnott** is the bestselling author of the Gone Viking travelogues and Season memoirs (*A Season on Vancouver Island*, *A Season in the Okanagan*, and the forthcoming *A Festive Season on Vancouver Island*), and *A Perfect Day for a Walk: The History, Cultures, and Communities of Vancouver, on Foot*. The recipient of a Fellowship at London's Royal Geographical Society for his expeditions, Bill is a frequent presenter and contributor to universities, podcasts, magazines, TV, and radio. When not trekking with a small pack and journal, Bill can be found on Canada's west coast, where he lives near the sea on Musqueam, Squamish, and Tsleil-Waututh land. ♣

We would like to take this opportunity to acknowledge the Traditional Territories upon which we live and work. In Calgary, Alberta, we acknowledge the Niitsítapi (Blackfoot) and the people of the Treaty 7 region in Southern Alberta, which includes the Siksika, the Piikuni, the Kainai, the Tsuut'ina, and the Stoney Nakoda First Nations, including Chiniki, Bearpaw, and Wesley First Nations. The City of Calgary is also home to Métis Nation of Alberta, Region III. In Victoria, British Columbia, we acknowledge the Traditional Territories of the Lkwungen (Esquimalt and Songhees), Malahat, Pacheedaht, Scia'new, T'Sou-ke, and W̱SÁNEĆ (Pauquachin, Tsartlip, Tsawout, Tseycum) Peoples.